RISK MANAGEMENT

- SIMPLIFIED -

A DEFINITIVE GUIDE FOR WORKPLACE AND PROCESS RISK MANAGEMENT

Sonni Gopal

CMIOSH CEng CEnvSoc SFIIRSM FIChemE

Copyright and Disclaimer

Dedication

To the 3 most important people in my life who have always kept me grounded:

My Wife (Amar), Son (Rav) and Daughter (Sukh)

Table of Contents

Preface

I have been involved with workplace and process risk management for over 30 years and I have always found the subject fascinating and rewarding. However, I am still surprised at the lack of deep understanding within Organisations about risk management.

Regardless of Organisation size, many see it as just "managing risks" because it's easier to explain and perhaps reactionary since it has the word "management".

Risk management is more than just "managing risks". Successful risk management requires a holistic approach based upon **Elements** that make up a Risk Management Framework.

Let's pretend you are my Client and I've asked you these 7 questions:

1. Do you know the relationship between attitude and risk management?

2. Do you know how to control workplace and process risks?

3. Do you know the difference between hazard identification and risk assessment?

4. Do you know what or who is a risk owner?

5. Do you know what you are measuring for successful risk management?

6. Do you know what or when you are monitoring for risk management?

7. Do you know what to do when reviewing risk management?

Did you answer "YES" to all of them? If you did, you don't need this book.

If you had even just one "NO" as an answer, this book is worth reading.

This is a reference book and not a novel. In this book, risk management is focused on **workplace and process related risks.** However, the approach and techniques can be applied for risk management generally.

My goal is to share valuable lessons learnt and my experience of getting risk management successfully embedded within your Organisation. My intended audiences are risk and safety management practitioners, trainers, managers, leaders in Organisations and anyone interested in successfully managing risks.

Unfortunately, a book of this size can't cover all the different ways of planning and delivering risk management. However, it can provide you with a stepping-stone for further exploration and development.

I hope that all those who use this book will find it insightful and helpful.

Thank you.

Sonni Gopal (2019)

CHAPTER 1: BASELINE

1.1 Icons Used in this Book

Icons are a great way to not only draw attention but also offer guidance.

I have used the following icons in this book:

Icons Used in this Book

Icon	Meaning	Description
	Template	Discussion feature or suggested format for document content.
	Reminder	Useful to commit to memory (or jot down for future quick reference)
	Tip	Based on experience and useful for future reference.
	Caution	Common mistakes, traps and pitfalls.
	Example	An example based upon experience and/or lessons learned.

1.2 Conventions and Assumptions

Assumptions made and conventions adopted are as follows.

Conventions and Assumptions

Conventions	Assumptions
Throughout this book the use of words, grammar and spelling are based upon British preference. For example: • Use of **Standardisation** instead of **Standardization**. • Use of **Organisation** instead of **Organization**	I had to make some assumptions (about my readers) as follows: • You have an active interest in reducing workplace and process risks within your Organisation. • You are familiar with Standards, policies, procedures etc within an Organisational context. • You are familiar with Health, Safety and Environment (HSE) fundamentals. • You want to apply risk management principles at an individual or Organisational level I.e., you are interested in the mechanics of risk management.

1.3 Book Logic

Unfortunately, there are no "magic bullets" when it comes to risk management within an Organisation. **Not even in this book**!

Undesirable consequences are often the result of inadequate risk management processes. Successful risk management requires a structured framework, clear direction, intent, expectations and agreed requirements.

In this book, I start with some fundamental requirements for alignment. We then dive deeper into the Risk Management Framework, work our way through the Risk Management Policy and then explore the Risk Management Plan.

In the Risk Management Plan, we look at the various Elements that work together to deliver the Plan.

- There are numerous books and literature available for risk management. I have minimised using and citing references to other works and authors because my preference is using standards published by the International Organisation for Standardisation (ISO).

ISO Standards require majority consensus of approval by at least 75% of the member bodies casting a vote. This provides a level of assurance that verification is thorough. Using ISO Standards as a reference has a strong foundation.

- As you read this book, you will notice that I keep repeating definitions.
- I make no apology for this because my

intention is to ensure that these definitions remain prominent.

- It's only by repetition that I can emphasise the importance of committing these definitions to the memory cells.

OK…if you are anything like me, **you just want the juicy bits.**

Let's begin.

1.4 The ISO 31000 Risk Management Standard

To a large extent, I have referenced the Risk Management Framework as defined in the ISO31000 Standard for Risk Management.

The ISO 31000 Standard is a good source for Organisations who want to follow a recognised international framework regarding setting up, evaluating and further improving their risk management arrangements.

 ISO Standards require majority consensus of approval by at least 75% of the member bodies casting a vote. This provides a level of assurance that verification is thorough. Using ISO Standards as a reference has a strong foundation.

In any case, there is no need to rush out and buy these Standards as throughout this book my intention is to **simplify** Risk Management and I will take into consideration the International approach and industry best practice.

- Standards change periodically based on review cycles etc. Keep in touch with such Standards, especially if you adopt them for your Organisation.

- It is also wise to ensure that there is a Standards review and update process in place.

You can purchase the Standard and get further information from the ISO Website**[3]**.

1.5 Important Key Definitions

As we know, the International Organisation for Standardisation (ISO) have some important Standards associated with risk management. Terminology and definitions from these Standards (and other relevant sources) used in this book are referenced in the table below.

Important Key Definitions

Terminology	Definition
Ref: ISO 31000 (2018) - Risk Management Principles and Guidelines	
Consequences	Outcome of an event affecting objectives
Event	Occurrence or change of a particular set of circumstances.
Likelihood	Chance of something happening.
Residual Risk	Risk remaining after risk treatment (I.e., process to modify the risk).
Review	Activity undertaken to determine the suitability, adequacy and effectiveness of the subject matter to achieve established objectives.
Risk	Risk is a combination of the consequences (I.e., outcome) of an event (including changes in circumstances) and the associated chance of something happening (I.e., likelihood or probability)
Risk Analysis	Process to comprehend the nature of risk and to determine the level of risk.
Risk Assessment	Overall process of risk identification, risk analysis and risk evaluation.
Risk Attitude	Organisation's approach to assess and eventually pursue, retain, take or turn away from risk.
Risk Control	Measure (or process) that is modifying the risk.
Risk Criteria	Terms of reference against which the

Terminology	Definition
	significance of a risk is evaluated.
Risk Evaluation	Process of comparing results of the risk analysis with Risk Criteria to determine whether the risk and/or its magnitude is acceptable or tolerable.
Risk Identification	Process of finding, recognising and describing risks.
Risk Level	Magnitude of risk or combination of risks, expressed in terms of the combination of consequences and their likelihood.
Risk Management	Coordinated activities to direct and control an Organisation with regard to risk.
Risk Management Framework	Set of components that provide the foundations and Organisational arrangements for designing, implementing, monitoring, reviewing and continually improving risk management throughout the Organisation.
Risk Management Plan	Scheme within the risk management framework specifying the approach, the management components and resources to be applied to the management of risk.
Risk Management Policy	Statement of the overall intentions and direction of an Organisation related to risk management.
Risk Owner	Person or entity with the accountability and authority to manage a risk.
Risk Profile	Description of any set of risks
Risk Treatment	Process to modify risk.
Risk Treatment Plan	Purpose is to document how the chosen treatment options will be implemented
Stakeholder	Person or Organisation that can affect, be affected by, or perceive themselves to be affected by a decision or activity.
Ref: ISO Guide 73 (2009) - Risk Management Vocabulary	
Risk Appetite	Amount and type of risk that an

Terminology	Definition
	Organisation is willing to pursue or retain.
Risk Perception	Stake holder's view on a risk.
Risk Tolerance	An Organisation's or stockholder's readiness to bear the risk after risk treatment in order to achieve its objectives

Ref: ISO 45001 (2018) - Occupational Health and Safety Management Systems

Terminology	Definition
Hazard	Source with a potential to cause injury and ill health.
Organisation	Person or group of people that has its own functions with responsibilities, authorities and relationships to achieve its objectives.
Process	Set of interrelated or interacting activities which transforms inputs and outputs.
Workplace	Place under the control of the Organisation where a person needs to be or to go for work purposes.

Ref: Organisation for Economic Co-operation and Development (OECD)[4]

Terminology	Definition
Key Risk Indicator (KRI)	An indicator that estimates the potential for some form of resource degradation using mathematical formulae or models.

- There is no need to memorise all these definitions…!

- To minimise going back and forth, I will repeat the definitions, when needed.

CHAPTER 2: THE RISK MANAGEMENT FRAMEWORK

2.1 Setting the Scene

When I visit any Organisation, a question that I often ask is "do you have a Risk Management Framework?"

The response, nearly always, is a resounding "yes, of course". I then follow up with my next question, which is "how do you manage your risks?"

Even with large Organisations, I am surprised at the responses that I receive.

Sure enough, responses start logical but soon turn into jargon and waffle. There is a sort of a beginning and an end, but everything in between is either grey or just "fill in the missing bits".

In reality, I should neither be shocked nor surprised. There is a lot of confusion in the ether, mostly propelled by misinterpretation.

- The aim of this book is to **simplify risk management**.

- I want to do this by applying the experiences and lessons learnt over my 30-year career in risk management.

- My approach is based on practical and successful application. **Why re-invent the wheel?**

During our journey together, I will:

- Define risk, hazard and other key definitions centred around risk management.

- Set some context and baseline regarding the size of an Organisation.

- Provide clarity and guidance on the Risk Management Framework and components such as the Risk Management Policy and Risk Management Plan.

- Elaborate and simplify the critical Elements associated with the Risk Management Plan.

- Share some closing thoughts for going forward.

Risk management is an iterative process.

If you come across ways that are effective and work for you and your Organisation don't discard them. Build on them and incorporate some (if not all) of the principles outlined within this book.

Remember, it's the start of your Risk Management journey and hopefully not the end!

Does the size of my Organisation matter?

2.2 Size Does Matter

We are all familiar with Organisation size and when it comes to risk management, **Size Does Matter.**

Typically, Organisation size relates to being Small, Medium or Large, especially in conversational terms.

Small and Medium-sized Enterprises (SMEs) are defined in the EU recommendation 2003/361 and the latter also includes an additional category known as "Micro"**[5]**.

The table below provides an overview (using Euro's as the monetary value):

Organisation Size Defined

Company Category	Staff Headcount	Turnover	Balance Sheet Total
Medium	< 250	≤ € 50 m	≤ € 43 m
Small	< 50	≤ € 10 m	≤ € 10 m
Micro	< 10	≤ € 2 m	≤ € 2 m

The 2 key factors that define the size of an Organisation (or enterprise) are:
1. **Number of employees** (or staff headcount); and
2. **Organisation's finances** (I.e., Turnover or Balance Sheet Total)

 Using the above figures, the size of the Organisation can be defined. This is a useful baseline for comparative analysis with other similar Organisations (e.g., for performance improvement, which we will cover later).

Typically, the larger the Organisation, the larger the risk portfolio and the potential impact of risks.

2.3 What is Risk and the Risk Equation?

Surprise, surprise…I am going to use the word "risk" a lot in this book, as expected.

What exactly is risk…is there an equation?

Risk is defined as:

A combination of the consequences (I.e., outcome) of an event (including changes in circumstances) and the associated chance of something happening (I.e., likelihood or probability). Let's expand on this further.

As a noun or verb, risk can be described as:

- A situation involving exposure to danger (**noun**); or

- Exposing (someone or something of value) to danger, harm, or loss (**verb**).

A good interpretation of **etymology** of risk (by Rolf Skjong) is based on the story of Odysseus sailing through the Strait of Messina[6].

When Odysseus had to sail through the Strait of Messina between Italy and Sicily, he was in a predicament and had 2 options:
1. Avoid the monster Scylla living on the rocky cliffs of Italy - the consequence is that he and the men on his ship would be further endangered in becoming swallowed whole by Charybdis, the whirlpool off the coast of Sicily.
2. Avoid the whirlpool Charybdis - the consequence is that he would inadvertently be pushing himself and the men on his ship closer towards Scylla, making it easier for

the monster to swallow all the men on the ship.

This story might be the origin of the phrase, "between a rock and a hard place".

Risks can be **Internal** or **External** facing.

Internal risks are those that you can predict, plan for and control (within moderation) as shown with examples in the table below.

Internal Facing Risks

Human	Factors can include employees, vendors and customers.
Technological	Factors include computers, information technology and business processes that rely on technology to remain cost-effective and efficient
Physical factors	Include equipment malfunctions, downtime and eventual obsolescence

Not always business-specific, **external risks** are those over which you have little or no control as shown with examples in the table below.

External Facing Risks

Country risk	A country will not be able to honour its financial commitments.
Political risk	The risk of political instability or changes in a country
Market risk	The risk that an investment will lose financial value due to market forces.

Unfortunately, in the world of risk management, nothing is straight forward!

But let's keep it simple.

In its simplest form, we can consider risk in the following equation format:

Risk = [Consequence] * [Likelihood]

There are variations and complex versions of the above equation, including weighting etc. For our purposes (keeping it simple), I will use the above equation throughout the book.

The Risk Equation:

Risk = [Consequence] * [Likelihood]

2.4 Hazard and Risk - What's the Difference?

It can be somewhat confusing because the terms **Hazard** and **Risk** are often used interchangeably, but in fact, they are unique expressions.

We know that risk is defined as:

A combination of the consequences (I.e., outcome) of an event (including changes in circumstances) and the associated chance of something happening (I.e., likelihood or probability).

But, what about a hazard?

Hazard is defined as:

Source with a potential to cause injury and ill health (I.e., a source with a consequence)

The following examples will help to clarify:

- If there was a spill of water in a room then that water would present a slipping hazard to people passing over it (i.e., the **consequence** is causing harm).
- If access to that area was prevented by a physical barrier then the hazard would remain but the risk would be reduced (i.e., the **likelihood** is reduced)

Therefore, for risk to be present there must be a hazard and a likelihood of occurrence.

We can now do some substitution of words and have an additional dimension to our Risk Equation, as follows:

Risk Equation:

Risk = [Consequence] * [Likelihood]
Risk = [Consequence] * [Likelihood] = [Hazard] * [Likelihood]

Hence, the difference between a Hazard and Risk is that:

- A hazard is something that can cause injury and ill health.
- Risk is the likelihood of realising a hazard.

2.5 What is Risk Management?

Risk Management is defined as:

Coordinated activities to direct and control an Organisation with regard to risk.

Sounds straight forward…right?

In my experience, when it comes to risk management, there are two types of Organisations:

- The "**box-tickers**" - they have a list with checkboxes that they tick items off to show done or completed; and

- Those with a **framework** - they have a structured risk management process to improve decision-making and drive performance.

Which one does your Organisation prescribe to, somewhere in between maybe?

At the beginning of this book, I mentioned that Organisations generally say, "**we do risk management**". This is a fair response because Organisations are reasonably aware of risks and they do tend to operate somewhere in the middle zone (i.e., a process with checklists that they use for verification etc).

However, the follow-up question about "**defining risk management**" provides emphasis on a bias (i.e., box-ticking or structured approach). The Organisation's response will give me an indication of where they place their Organisation on the risk management spectrum.

Organisations understand what risks there are within their operations. However, they may not be able to fully articulate what exactly risk management means in the holistic sense (i.e., **Risk Management Framework**). Risk management is about "coordinated activities" associated with the Risk Management Framework.

2.6 What is the Risk Management Framework?

The Risk Management Framework forms part of an Organisation's strategic and operational policies and practices.

Risk Management Framework is defined as:

 Set of components that provide the foundations and Organisational arrangements for designing, implementing, monitoring, reviewing and continually improving risk management throughout the Organisation.

We can add more granularity to the above definition as follows:

Risk Management Framework

Specifics	Foundations	Arrangements
Alternative	Risk Management Policy **{Policy}**	Risk Management Plan **{Plan}**
	<u>**Definition:**</u> ✓ High-level statement of the overall intentions and direction of an Organisation related to risk management.	<u>**Definition:**</u> ✓ Scheme specifying the approach, the management components (or elements) and resources to be applied to the management of risk.
	<u>**Comprises:**</u> • Sets out the objectives, mandate, roles, responsibilities and	<u>**Comprises:**</u> • Procedures • Treatment plans • Assignment of responsibilities • Performance measurement

Specifics	Foundations	Arrangements
	commitment to manage risk. • Provides an overview of the Risk Management Framework and Plan.	• Monitoring and reporting • Review periods. • Sequence and timing of activities

For our purposes, we can consider:

Risk Management Framework = Foundations + Arrangement

Risk Management **Framework** = Risk Management **Policy** + Risk Management **Plan**

There are various factors that can influence risk within risk management.

2.7 What Factors Influence Risk Management?

Factors that influence risk and risk management varies between Organisations and even between Organisations in the same sector.

- Several books and research papers have been written by distinguished authors about risk **influencing factors**. *Unfortunately, some are very confusing and in repeat mode, focusing more on quantity rather than quality.*

- If in doubt, refer to International Standards as your first option.

From a helicopter view perspective, influencing factors associated with risk management includes the following:

Risk Elements and Influencing Factors

Element	Influencing Factors
1. Attitude	Appetite for risk (i.e., aversion, seeker or neutral)
2. Control	Activities or tools that modify the risk (I.e., process, policy, device, practice or other actions).
3. Identification and Assessment	Hazard profile (i.e., description of hazards within the Organisation, internal and external). Risk analysis (or evaluation) criteria and rule set specific to the Organisation
4. Actions Management	Acceptance and commitment to track, follow up, assign resources etc..
5. Performance Improvement	Monitoring & Measurement programmes, Key Performance Indicator (KPI) requirements.
6. Review	Commitment (i.e., audits and/or inspections and follow up)

- We are going to cover each Element above in much more detail when we discuss Risk Management Plans.

- At this stage, my intention is to provide you with an introduction to influence and how risks are accepted, appreciated or rejected within Organisations.

Let's play devils' advocate on the above factors for your Organisation.

- Within your Organisation, you might propose that "it's more about people's attitude to risk".

- See how the other elements weigh in…did it change your perspective?

2.8 Why Manage Risks?

There is a level of uncertainty in everything that we do especially as things don't always go to plan.

We don't always get 100% of the desired outcome. Even if we did, perhaps there was an element of luck involved?

Given the choice, Organisations would much prefer to operate with "zero" risk. But, that's just a pipe dream.

There are always risks that an Organisation will **never** be able to manage or control related to political issues, exchange rates, interest rates and so on.

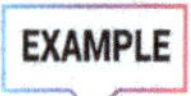

At the time of writing this book, one of the biggest drivers of uncertainty in the UK is Brexit. Organisations are swimming in a mud-pool of unknowns due to of a lack of clarity on what the future landscape will look like for trading and economic stability.

Risks generate uncertainty and uncertainty is just like "Kryptonite" for any Organisation.

Kryptonite:
It originates from the fictional world of Cartoons, TV and Film for the character Superman.
Kryptonite is a mineral from Superman's ancestral planet, Krypton. It was the only thing that could be used to either hurt or kill Superman.

Taking uncertainty further, the "**Domino**" **(Heinrich,1931)** and "**Swiss Cheese**" **(Reason, 1990)** models are widely used to show how failure (or a sequence of failures) can result in occurrence and cascading events.

The table below illustrates the concepts.

Risk Models

Domino Effect (Heinrich, 1931)	Swiss Cheese (Reason, 1990)
A simple type of model highlighting the "cascade" concept or chain reaction.	There might be several layers of protection (cheese slices), but when all the "holes" line up, it results in an undesirable outcome due to a hazard (I.e., harm in the above image).

Understanding how risks manifest in your Organisation provides essential and critical input for successful risk management. It provides a moderate degree of certainty.

Some Organisations are very good at managing their risks using bespoke analytical and forecasting tools that they have developed over time. This gives them a positive advantage in relation to certainty.

On the flip side, **some Organisations are terrible**. Suffering from "**paralysis by analysis**" or living in the moment, hoping that they will survive. They are not even sure about certainty in the present, never mind the future.

 Understanding and managing internal and wherever possible external risks, provides an Organisation significant opportunity to minimise exposure to their Kryptonite.

 Previously, you may recall, we discussed internal and external risks (Ref: What is Risk and the Risk Equation).

Let's not forget that within **internal** and **external** risks there are also various types e.g., financial, security, operational, safety etc.

With such choice and variety, we **must be very specific when we discuss risks and risk management**.

2.9 What Type of Risk Does this Book Focus On?

Risks come in all shapes, sizes and with different labels.

Whilst the concepts and methods outlined in this book can be readily applied to other risk types, this book primarily focuses on <u>**workplace and process risks**</u>.

You will recall that Risk is defined as:

 A combination of the consequences (I.e., outcome) of an event (including changes in circumstances) and the associated chance of something happening (I.e., likelihood or probability).

We also have definitions for workplace and process as follows:

 <u>Workplace</u>
Place under the control of the Organisation where a person needs to be or to go for work purposes

<u>Process</u>
Set of interrelated or interacting activities which transforms inputs and outputs.

By combination, we can, therefore, conclude the following:

Workplace and Process Risks Defined

Workplace Risk	Process Risk
Consequences (I.e., outcome) of an event (including changes in circumstances) and the associated chance of something happening (I.e., likelihood or probability) in a place under the control of the Organisation, where a person	Consequences (I.e., outcome) of an event (including changes in circumstances) and the associated chance of something happening (I.e., likelihood or probability) associated with a set of

Workplace Risk	Process Risk
needs to be or to go for work purposes	interrelated or interacting activities which transforms inputs and outputs.

Managing workplace and process related risks minimise the effects of shocks and stresses in a place of work and activities therein (i.e., **future proofing**).

Further rational behind the significance of managing workplace and process risks are outlined in the table below.

Workplace and Process Risks Overview

Why Workplace Risk?	Why Process Risk?
Someday in the future, Artificial Intelligence (AI) will allow Organisational activities to be managed either remotely or autonomously. Till then, activities are reliant on manual labour or facilitated via automation. The common denominator in every Organisation is "people". People go to work and can potentially be exposed to **internal** risks within the Organisation.	Processes take place within an Organisation because input results in an output. No input means no output, no Organisation and no risk. Whilst not commercially lucrative, this would be a Utopian risk avoidance solution. Process operation, maintenance, fault fixing, technological innovation and other factors all add to the hazard profile of an Organisation. History is littered with catastrophic events as a result of poorly managed process risks.

With our focus firmly fixed on **workplace and process related risks**, we need a supporting framework for achieving our Organisation's risk management objectives.

We established that our Risk Management Framework can be defined as:

Risk Management Framework = Foundations + Arrangements…or

Risk Management **Framework** = Risk Management **Policy** + Risk Management **Plan**

CHAPTER 3: RISK MANAGEMENT POLICY

3.1 Introduction to the Risk Management Policy

The Risk Management Policy is a fundamental part of the Organisation's Risk Management Framework.

The Risk Management Policy is defined as:

Statement of the overall intentions and direction of an Organisation related to risk management.

We know that our:

Risk Management Framework = Foundations + Arrangements... or

Risk Management **Framework** = Risk Management **Policy** + Risk Management **Plan**

It is highly likely that your Organisation will have its own bespoke format and content for policies and care should be taken to not negate existing processes and practices.

The primary intention of the Risk Management Policy is to endorse and support a framework for the management of risk. It is also a stament of commitment to increase overall awareness of risk throughout the Organisation.

To facilitate the above:

- The Risk Management Policy is a declaration of commitment and is therefore endorsed by

the highest level within the Organisation by the **Risk Owner(s)**.

- The intention is to increase awareness of **ownership**, commitment, responsibilities and enforcement.

Ownership is not about closing actions by the **Risk Owner(s).**

3.2 Risk Owners and Ownership

A Risk Owner is defined as:

 Person or entity with the accountability and authority to manage a risk.

Ownership is <u>NOT</u> about closing actions.

Ownership is about having the accountability and authority to manage risks by (but not limited to):

- Facilitating and supporting in the development, implementation and maintenance of the Risk Management Framework for managing risk;

- Facilitating and supporting people in the Organisation with responsibility for the risk management process;

- Ensuring the adequacy, effectiveness and efficiency of any controls; and

- Establishing performance measurement, external and/or internal communication, reporting and escalation processes.

 The Organisation and/or Risk Owners may set their intention and direction out clearly by embedding their requirements within the Organisation's **Risk Management Policy**.

How do you develop your Risk Management Policy?

3.3 Developing a Risk Management Policy

The Risk Management Policy is defined as follows:

Person or entity with the accountability and authority to manage a risk.

We know that the purpose of a Risk Management Policy is to:

- Clearly, show a declaration of commitment by the **Risk Owners**.

- Increase awareness of **ownership**, commitment, responsibilities and enforcement.

Taking the above into consideration, the custodian of the Policy is generally the Risk Owner. Whilst responsibilities can be delegated, accountability will remain with the Risk Owner.

Therefore, when developing your Risk Management Policy do take into consideration the following:

- An overview of the risk management process (I.e., elements, components etc);

- Objectives and commitment;

- Roles and responsibilities to help ensure the risk management process is understood; and

- A summary or overview of the Risk Management Plan, which generally includes procedures, practices, assignment of responsibilities, sequence and timing of activities etc.

The above is just a snapshot. It can be modified as necessary to fit your Organisation's needs.

- Just like every other policy, it might sound straight forward. However, Risk Management Policies differ between Organisations because it can be relative to scale, nature of operations and complexity of the business.

- Your Risk Management Policy needs to be bespoke to your Organisation.

- Avoid **"copy and paste"**.

With the Risk Management Policy progressed, we can now focus our attention on the **Risk Management Plan**.

CHAPTER 4: RISK MANAGEMENT PLAN

4.1 Introduction to the Risk Management Plan

We now know that:

Risk Management Framework = Foundations + Arrangements… or

Risk Management **Framework** = Risk Management **Policy** + Risk Management **Plan**

Now progressed, our Risk Management Policy is "fundamental" and reasonably straight forward to understand. On the other hand, the Risk Management Plan (or "arrangements") is a little more demanding in terms of development.

The Risk Management Plan is defined as:

Scheme within the Risk Management Framework specifying the approach, the management components and resources to be applied to the management of risk.

Forming part of the Risk Management Framework, the Risk Management Plan provides the architecture to ensure that risks have been addressed as prescribed by the Organisation. We can think of the architecture in the Risk Management Plan as having several **Elements**.

In Chapter 2 (The Risk Management Framework), I made reference to the Risk Management Plan and provided a short overview in tabular format, as follows:

Risk Management Plan Overview

Specifics	Arrangements
Alternative	Risk Management Plan {Plan}
	**Definition:** Scheme specifying the approach, the management components (or Elements) and resources to be applied to the management of risk.
	Comprises: • Procedures • Treatment plans • Assignment of responsibilities • Performance measurement • Monitoring and reporting • Review periods. • Sequence and timing of activities

There is no specific format for a Risk Management Plan.

Generally, it's a case of what works best for your Organisation. Some can be very detailed and have rolled up treatment plans, risks register etc.

- Simplicity is the key to success for Risk Management Plans.
- The intention is to communicate to the highest level within your Organisation, this means keep it succinct, factual and precise.

The Risk Management Plan approach in this book is based on the following **Elements** that make up the architecture:

Risk Management Plan Elements

Description	Element
Defining the attitude within the Organisation	1. Attitude
Controlling risks	2. Control
Identifying hazards and assessing the risk.	3. Hazard Identification and Risk Assessment (HIRA)
Assigning responsibility for actions.	4. Actions Management
Measuring and monitoring performance	5. Performance Improvement
Reviewing performance for continuous improvement	6. Review

- Readers will note that I haven't included communication and training (as examples) in the above list of Elements. This doesn't mean they are not important (cf: Closing Thoughts Section at the end of the book).

- To cover these "other" aspects as Elements within this book will dilute the core requirements that are necessary for establishing the main architecture for the Risk Management Plan.

It's worth noting that many Organisations have specific aspects (e.g., communication, training) as part of other programmes such as Learning & Development, Competency, Communications etc.

Duplication is not necessary, but signposting is essential.

4.2 Do you need a Risk Management Procedure?

A question that I get asked often is "should I have a Risk Management Procedure?"

The purpose of a Risk Management Procedure is to set out clearly the framework and requirements for the management of risk within the Organisation.

The Risk Management Procedure is unique and intended to convey important information on "how to do something" in a structured way that has been approved by the Organisation's Risk Owners.

Typical components in your Risk Management Procedure will include (but not limited to):

- Purpose (or intent);

- Procedure ownership;

- Describing the Risk Management Framework, Policy and Plan (e.g., based upon the Elements described within this book);

- Defining responsibility and ownership aspects, including notification aspects (I.e., who needs to know). This is important if there are thousands of risk management actions;

- Describing the process or methodology for risk management (e.g., using a flowchart); and

- Describe actions management, record keeping, review etc.

The Risk Management Procedure can signpost to other relevant procedures that form part of the Risk Management Plan or other management systems (e.g., safety, environment).

Signposting can include:

- Hazard Identification and Risk Assessment (HIRA) procedure
- Performance measurement and monitoring procedure.
- Environmental Management System (ISO 14001)
- Safety Management System (ISO 45001).

Coming back to our question - do you need a Risk Management Procedure?

- This really depends on how much of a structure you have in place already.

- It's important to **not overburden** the Risk Management Procedure, especially when supporting documents can be referenced for additional information and guidance.

- Remember: **Duplication is not necessary, but signposting is essential**.

Our first **Element** to cover in the Risk Management Plan is Risk Attitude.

4.3 ELEMENT 1: Risk Attitude

E1.1 What's the Organisation's Risk Attitude?

Search on the Internet for "Risk Attitude" and you will find an endless stream of information discussing behaviours, psychological profiling, **gambling addiction** (!) and so on… you might even strike it lucky and find quality information on "Risk Attitude in an Organisation".

We are focusing on an Organisation's Risk Attitude. Risks within an Organisation are managed by a few but will impact many.

It's important for the Organisation to have the right Risk Attitude because it's pivotal in our Risk Management Framework. **But, why?**

Risk Attitude is defined as:

The Organisation's approach to assess and eventually pursue, retain, take or turn away from risk.

To facilitate focus on an Organisation's risk and attitude, we need to address the following 2 themes that drive Risk Attitude:

1. **Types**; and

2. **Motivators**.

In fact, the types and motivators we are going to discuss are just as applicable to people. **After all, Organisations are managed by people**.

E1.2 Types of Risk Attitude

Have you heard the expression "it's in the company's DNA"?

Alas, an Organisation is not a living entity with DNA etc. So, how can we know the Risk Attitude of an Organisation?

We defined Risk Attitude as:

The Organisation's approach to assess and eventually pursue, retain, take or turn away from risk.

Organisations have different attitudes towards risk due to uncertainty, which in turn affects the way they pursue, retain, take or turn away from risk.

For any Organisation to know what type of Risk Attitude they have (I.e., it's in their DNA), they first need to explore their risk motivators and the primary risk motivator within any Organisation is the Risk Owner.

A Risk Owner is defined as:

Person or entity with the accountability and authority to manage a risk.

Risk Owners are people (*some might disagree here*) and it's their personality and Risk Attitude that will be an imprint on the Organisation (I.e., the Organisation's Risk Attitude reflects the Risk Owner's Risk Attitude).

Organisations must, therefore, exhibit the following types of risk attitudes:

Risk Attitude Types Within Organisations

Risk Averse	Risk Neutral	Risk Seeking
Where an Organisation has a **negative bias towards uncertainty**. There is a greater focus on security and certainty with a view to reducing liability, stress and discomfort.	Where an Organisation's risk preference is **between the two extremes.** In reality, this may not be exactly 50:50 because the pendulum can swing in either direction between averse or seeking.	Where an Organisation has a **positive bias towards uncertainty**. There is a greater focus on maximising returns (e.g., financial) or other potential benefits (e.g., reduce the time for completing an activity).

I realise that the above might appear somewhat obvious. My intention was to emphasise the importance of Risk Owners and how much of an impact they have in shaping the Risk Attitude within their entire Organisation. **It's a ripple effect!**

To conclude:

- The Organisation is not a living entity, but the personality of the Risk Owner(s) and their Risk Attitude will be an imprint on the Organisation.

- It's important to **know and understand what motivates an Organisation's Risk Attitude**.

E1.3 What motivates Risk Attitude?

To answer the question "what motivates Risk Attitude", we need to backtrack to another question that we asked earlier, which was "**why manage risks?**"

Do you recall "**Kryptonite**"?

It originates from the fictional world of Cartoons, TV and Film for the character Superman. Kryptonite is a mineral from Superman's ancestral planet, Krypton. It was the only thing that could be used to either hurt or kill him.

Organisations exist in a real-world setting, not cartoons and they play a very important role in:

- Contributing to a Country's economic stability;

- Providing people with jobs, security (within moderation) and an income; and

- Generating worthwhile products and/or services.

Therefore, taking the above into consideration, factors that can motivate an Organisation's Risk Attitude will include the following:

Risk Attitude Motivators

Risk Attitude Motivators
● Financial (I.e., profitability)
● Transformational (I.e., life-changing)
● Cost Reducing (time and/or materials)
● Public Relations
● Legislation
● Stakeholders

Risk Attitude Motivators
● **Reducing Hazard (I.e., harm to people)**
● Reducing Environmental Impact

In the table above, I have bolded the **"Reducing Hazard"** text (I.e., harm to people) since we are focusing on workplace and process related risks and hazards.

Reducing hazards has to be a positive motivator because no Organisation sets out to intentionally harm people....**that's just crazy!**

Let's not forget that motivating factors can also:

- Provide a **Positive**, **Negative** or **Neutral** bias, depending on the circumstances and/or individuals concerned; and

- Be multi-faceted (I.e., impacts several categories).

For example:
- Financial - potential big gains.
- Security - in country terrorism issues.
- Public relations - huge media exposure.
- Harm to people - extends beyond the fence line; and
- Environmental impact - carbon footprint.

To ensure that your Organisation's motivators are aligned with its Risk Attitude:

- Take time to review and recognise what motivates the Organisation.

- Remember, it can be biased and multi-faceted.

E1.4 The Importance of Risk Attitude and Motivators

Risk Attitude is defined as:

 Organisation's approach to assess and eventually pursue, retain, take or turn away from risk.

William Blake (famous English poet) said:

"Hindsight is a wonderful thing but foresight is better, especially when it comes to saving a life, or some pain".

With Mr Blake in mind, ask the following questions about your Organisation's Risk Attitude motivators.

Questions to Ask About Your Organisation's Risk Attitude Motivators

Baseline	Past & Present (Hindsight)	Future (Foresight)
Organisation size and Complexity	• Do you know the size of your Organisation?	• Relative to size, do you have any thoughts or views on where you want to be in 3, 5 or 10 years from now?
Risk Attitude	• Do you know what is your Organisation's Risk Attitude? • Are you reasonably happy with the Risk Attitude? • If not, what can	• Will your "right now" Risk Attitude support future Organisation size and growth requirements? • If not, what can you do to improve?

Baseline	Past & Present (Hindsight)	Future (Foresight)
	you do to improve?	
Risk Attitude Motivators	• Do you know what are your Organisation's risk motivators (I.e., financial, health, wellbeing, security etc)? • Are you reasonably happy with your Risk Attitude motivators? • If appropriate or necessary, can your Risk Attitude be improved?	• For future growth aspirations, will your current set of motivators support your Risk Attitude requirements? • If not, what can you do to improve motivation?

- Understanding your Organisation's Risk Attitude provides an insight into how the Organisation will deal with risks (I.e., **averse, neutral or seeking).**

- Knowing the Organisation's Risk Attitude motivators plays a crucial role in deciding what to do with a risk (I.e., **pursue, retain, take or turn away from risk**).

<u>For example</u>:
- The Organisation might be risk seeking because it is highly motivated due to financial gain.

- However, there is a significantly higher risk due to the "new" chemicals being used because of potential exposure to people, fire and explosions.
- In this case, the Organisation might choose to turn away from the risk.

The above (simple) example illustrates some of the thought processes involved when taking decisions on risks. They form part of a rule set or rules of engagement, or more commonly known as **Risk Criteria**.

Risk Criteria is defined as:

Terms of reference against which the significance of a risk is evaluated.

Understanding what motivates your Organisation's Risk Attitude is a critical input in developing and embedding Risk Criteria for your Organisation.

We are going to cover Risk Criteria in much more detail in Element 3 when we discuss Hazard Identification and Risk Assessment (HIRA).

My intention here is to "**nudge**" you to start thinking about Risk Attitude, risk motivators and Risk Criteria. They are all very important foundations within your Risk Management Framework.

- Don't get too deep into thinking about Risk Criteria.
- We are going to cover Risk Criteria in much more detail when we review Hazard Identification and Risk Assessment (HIRA) in Element 3.

Before we progress from Risk Attitude, we need to discuss **Risk Attitude** and **Risk Tolerance.** Readers will be familiar with both these terms; however, they are both very different.

E1.5 Risk Attitude and Risk Tolerance

"But what about risk tolerance?", I hear you say…

Readers will have noticed that I prefer to use **Risk Attitude** throughout this book instead of **Risk Tolerance**…but why?

Tolerance **is not explicitly defined in ISO 31000 (2018)** but it is mentioned in the ISO Guide 73 (2009) as follows:

An Organisation's or Stockholder's readiness to bear the risk after risk treatment in order to achieve its objectives.

By referring to Risk Attitude, I know that I am maintaining continuity with the Risk Management Framework as prescribed in ISO 31000.

You may recall I mentioned that:

ISO Standards *require majority consensus of approval by at least 75% of the member bodies casting a vote. This provides a level of assurance on verification. Using ISO Standards as a reference has a strong foundation.*

In addition to the above, there are also other issues with using risk tolerability, such as:

For Example:

- Tolerable…..by whose standards?

- Does tolerable mean we don't have to do anything more?

- If tolerable, what's the value that we are placing on human life?

- There are various schools of thought regarding Risk Tolerance.
- I suspect I may have opened a can of worms here, especially in relation to the ISO 31000 Standard.

- My suggestion is "**the choice is yours**".
- I have included both ISO references in the interest of clarity.

Having understood Risk Attitude, established our risk motivators for the Organisation, we can now turn our attention to how we are going to **Control** risks.

4.4 ELEMENT 2: Control

E2.1 How Can We Control Risks?

Risk Control is defined as:

Measure (or process) that is modifying the risk.

Have you seen the "famous" picture of an iceberg with reference to safety or risk?

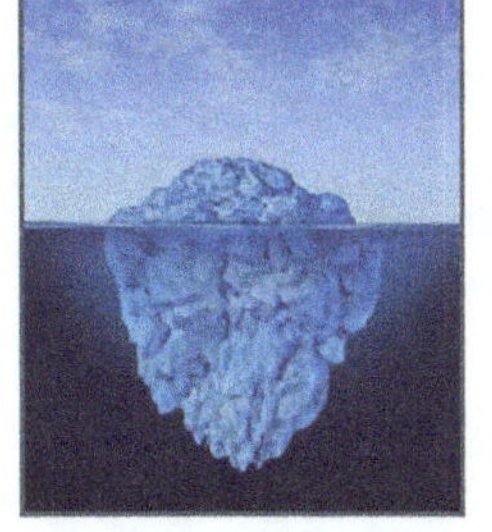

It's the picture of an iceberg with the premise being that hidden danger lurks below the water line.

What you see above the water line is only a small part of the frozen mountain under the sea.

Keep that "iceberg" picture in your mind for now…

Our Risk Equation is:

Risk = [Consequence] * [Likelihood]
Risk = [Consequence] * [Likelihood] = [Hazard] * [Likelihood]

From this equation, we can see that there are 2 inputs we can adjust or manipulate to change the outcome of risk.

We can modify or treat:

- The consequence; and /or

- The chance of occurrence.

By looking beneath the water line we can (to a certain extent) change the outcome of risk by applying control measures.

E2.2 What are Risk Control Measures?

We know that consequence and likelihood are the variables in our Risk Equation.

Risk = [Consequence] * [Likelihood]
Risk = [Consequence] * [Likelihood] = [Hazard] * [Likelihood]

Hence, there are possibilities in our favour that will allow us to reduce the consequence and/or the likelihood of occurrence. We can "control" the outcome of risk by:

- Reducing consequence **or** likelihood.

- Reducing consequence **and** likelihood.

- **Removing** the hazard completely.

The above "**sliding scale**" suggests that we could potentially have a "**hierarchy of control**" that can be applied for each risk.

- Removing the hazard completely is a great option because it gives zero risk.

- However, this might not be a viable option in some cases, because zero risks might mean zero input and subsequently zero output.

- Organisations must be careful in their selection of control measures. Some choices may also reveal a range of other potential risks that they might overlook (i.e., below the water line).

From the above, we take note that the Organisation may <u>have to accept some risks</u> regardless of consequence and/or likelihood not being favourable or acceptable relative to their Risk Criteria.

With a **hierarchy of control,** the Organisation can establish a "desirability" preference. Of course, this preference is significantly influenced by the Organisation's Risk Attitude and Risk Criteria.

Typically, relative to the "desirability" preference, the following options are available:

Hierarchy of Control Measures

Desirability Preference	Control Measure
1. The most desirable option	Elimination
2.	Substitution
3.	Isolation
4.	Engineering
5.	Administrative
6. The least desirable option	Personal Protective Equipment (PPE)

The above list can be modified, if necessary. However, the list presented is typical, widely accepted and considered adequate.

You can choose more than one:

- If one control measure is not enough to minimise the risk to an acceptable level, then a combination might work.

- Apply control measures one at a time to gauge the impact on the risk outcome.

- It's important to keep applying control measures until the risk becomes acceptable relative to the Organisation's Risk Criteria.

E2.3 Application of Risk Control Measures

In the previous section, based upon the desirability preference, we developed our **hierarchy of control measures** as follows:

Hierarchy of Control Measures

Desirability Preference	Control Measure
1. The most desirable option	Elimination
2.	Substitution
3.	Isolation
4.	Engineering
5.	Administrative
6. The least desirable option	Personal Protective Equipment (PPE)

Our focus is **workplace and process risks**.

Let's add another column labelled "Options" and in this new column, let's describe what we can do relative to that control measure, as given below:

Hierarchy of Control Measures with Options

Desirability Preference	Control	Options
1. The most desirable option	Elimination	• Eliminate the hazard. • No hazard no risk. • Remove the hazard.
2.	Substitution	• Replacing a hazardous substance • Replace process with a less hazardous

Desirability Preference	Control	Options
		one.
3.	Isolation	• Restricting access to plant and equipment or in the case of substances locking them away under strict controls.
4.	Engineering	• Redesign a process or piece of equipment to make it less hazardous. • Isolating the hazard from the person at risk.
5.	Administrative	• Implementing procedures, instructions or information sheets. • Providing appropriate training.
6. **The least desirable option**	Personal Protective Equipment (PPE)	• Providing PPE.

The above table adds a little more granularity, however, let's see it in action with an example.

Hierarchy of Control Measures with Options and Application Example

Use of Circular Bench Saw

In this example we are reviewing the use of a circular bench saw where the hazard is an injury to the operator.

What can we do to reduce the consequence (injury) and/or likelihood (chance)?

After review and brainstorming, the options for risk treatment proposed are as follows:

Order Preference	Control	Options
1. **The most desirable option**	Elimination	• Buy finished planks directly from the supplier so that cutting is not done on site.
2.	Substitution	• Use a hand saw instead of a circular saw. However, there are potential ergonomic issues that will require review ("**iceberg**" again).
3.	Isolation	• Limit the number of people exposed by only allowing one specified person to use the saw. • Barrier off the area where bench circular saw is to be used
4.	Engineering	• Install a large red protruding stop button that can be operated by the

Order Preference	Control	Options
		knee.
5.	Administrative	<ul><li>Procedure to be written instructing the operator to keep fingers clear of the saw blade.</li><li>Increased or better supervision - more frequent visits, more experienced supervision.</li><li>Identification of special training needs information/ instructions, labelling, posters, checklists. e.g. warning sign by bench saw, regular visits by supervision to ensure control measures enforced (e.g. guard not removed)</li></ul>
6. **The least desirable option**	Personal Protective Equipment	<ul><li>Bench circular saw operator to wear thick gloves (PPE).</li></ul>

<u>Remember to ask yourself:</u>
- What would be your choice?
- Does it create any additional hazards?
- How would you go about endorsing the choice

you made?

- Have we treated the risk adequately to meet the Organisation's Risk Criteria?

Control measures play a critical role in risk treatment. When selecting and applying control measures, it's important to remember that:

- Their use and application must be selective relative to a hierarchy.

- One control measure might not be enough, however, start with one and review the impact on risk treatment.

- Impact on risk treatment is reviewed relative to the Organisation's Risk Criteria.

4.5 ELEMENT 3: Hazard Identification and Risk Assessment (HIRA)

E3.1 What is Hazard Identification and Risk Assessment (HIRA)?

Let's revisit our definitions and relationship between risk, hazard and consequence.

<u>Risk is defined as</u>:
A combination of the consequences (I.e., outcome) of an event (including changes in circumstances) and the associated chance of something happening (I.e., likelihood or probability).

<u>Hazard is defined as</u>:
A source with a potential to cause injury and ill health (I.e., a source with a consequence).

<u>Consequence is defined as</u>:
Outcome of an event affecting objectives.

<u>Our Risk Equation is</u>:
Risk = [Consequence] * [Likelihood] = [Hazard] * [Likelihood]

Central to our Risk Management Framework and Risk Equation is a structured and robust approach for identifying hazards and assessing risks.

Think about a car without an engine. Unfortunately, it will not get very far, unless it's going downhill of course!

Hazard Identification and Risk Assessment (HIRA) is the engine in our "risk management vehicle".

The table below offers a "split" overview on HIRA using the **6W's**:

HIRA Overview Using 6Ws.

6Ws	Hazard Identification (HI)	Risk Assessment (RA)
What?	The first stage of a risk assessment process.	Assess hazards identified relative to likelihood to determine risk level and what needs to be done if anything.
Why?	To identify workplace and process hazards and then put them forward for risk assessment.	To minimise exposure to risk, liability and any potential business-related impacts.
When?	Typically: • Conceptual - designing (early) stage. • Development - design available and operations decided. • Realisation - prior to commissioning. • Operational - or utilisation, prior to any changes. • Improvement - prior to any operational enhancements and associated changes. • Decommissioning - prior to mothballing, cessation or disposal.	
Where?	At the Organisation's discretion.	
Who?	Team effort via brainstorming.	
HoW?	Using specific methodology and tools	

E3.2 What Does HIRA Involve?

Hazard Identification and Risk Assessment (HIRA) reviews are usually carried out at the same time. In fact, it is advisable to do them at the same time for continuity and consistency.

HIRA is essentially a 2 Step process and involves:

- **Step 1: Hazard Identification** - using a structured approach, wherein the team identifies hazards.

- **Step 2: Risk Assessment** - the risk of each hazard identified is assessed and reviewed for acceptability.

 During each Step (*especially Step 2*), risk acceptability is based upon the Organisation's Risk Criteria. This is a crucial interface and we will cover this separately for each of the above steps in the upcoming sections.

There are also various HIRA processes and methodology, which we will also cover in later sections.

Suffice to say, whichever HIRA processes or methodology the Organisation adopts, that will determine requirements for enabling material.

A generic list of enabling material for a HIRA review will include:

HIRA Enabling Material

Enabling Material (typical)	Scope Coverage
Data and information - relates to historical information, current operations, design and engineering information etc.	• Hazard Identification • Risk Assessment

Enabling Material (typical)	Scope Coverage
Procedures and Documents	• Hazard Identification • Risk Assessment
Terms of Reference	• Hazard Identification
Criteria for facilitating discussion and supporting decisions.	• Risk Assessments
Checklists	• Hazard Identification
Recording Sheets	• Hazard Identification • Risk Assessment

- As mentioned, there are various HIRA processes or methodology available.

- Even offering a quick overview of each method has the potential of making this book cumbersome and confusing.

- I have elected to adopt a "**sniper**" approach for focusing on **workplace and process risk** management. This includes proposing a widely used hazard identification technique, which we will cover later in the section "Step 1 - Hazard Identification".

Regardless of whichever HIRA processes or methodology you decide to use, all HIRA reviews will require up to date and accurate information. Having a defined, written structured procedure will also facilitate the process.

E3.3 Do you need a HIRA Procedure?

A question I get asked often is "**do I need a HIRA Procedure?**"

The purpose of your HIRA procedure is to clearly set out the **framework and requirements for conducting Hazard Identification and Risk Assessment** within your Organisation.

Apart from instructing the HIRA review team on how to proceed with HIRA reviews, the procedure will also detail the Organisation's Risk Criteria requirements.

Typically, the content of a HIRA procedure will cover:

- Purpose (or intent).

- Procedure ownership.

- Key enabling document requirements (e.g., Terms of Reference)

- Describing the HIRA process I.e., tools and techniques (e.g., using a flowchart).

- Describe actions management, record keeping, review etc.

What if you already have a Risk Management Procedure…?

Previously, I mentioned that it's important to **not overburden** your Risk Management Procedure, especially when supporting documents can be referenced for additional information and guidance.

With procedures, ensure they are accounted for and signposted in relevant documents by taking into account referential integrity (I.e., cross-referencing is a closed loop).

- **Duplication is not necessary, but signposting is essential.**

- The HIRA procedure can signpost to other relevant procedures that form part of the Risk Management Plan or other management systems (e.g., safety, environment).

For example, signposts to:
- Risk Management Procedure.
- Performance measurement and monitoring procedure.
- Environmental Management System (ISO 14001)
- Safety Management System (ISO 45001).

So, should you have a HIRA procedure…?

- Depends on how much of a structure you have in place already.

- As with the Risk Management Procedure, it's important to **not overburden** the framework of the procedures.

- Signpost, don't duplicate.

E3.4 Information Sources for HIRA Reviews

Hazard Identification and Risk Assessment (HIRA) reviews facilitate an Organisation's decision-making process for managing workplace and process risks.

To facilitate the HIRA review, we need information. That information must be reliable, accurate and up to date. Poor quality or out of date information will not only make the risk assessment process meaningless but can mask and potentially downplay "real" risks.

The source and quality of information are critical because otherwise:
Garbage In = Garbage Out

When conducting the HIRA review, it's important to take into consideration:

- **Historical conditions** - what has gone wrong in the past?

- **Existing conditions** - what can go wrong now?

- **Future conditions** - what could go wrong?

In order to take the above conditions into consideration, the 2 following information sources are available for HIRA reviews:

- Historical Records; and

- Design or Engineering Documents.

Both sources provide unique input, as detailed below.

Since this book focuses on **workplace and process risks**, the details below are themed accordingly regarding information sources.

Historical Records

For historical records, Organisations have at their disposal a number of **internal and external** information sources for data harvesting.

Historical records such as past performance, incidents, accidents, process releases etc., all offer an insight into the potential for recurrence.

Whilst not all sources below may be relevant to your Organisation, the table below offers suggestions for potential sources (with some overlap) relative to your workplace and process related hazards.

HIRA Information Sources for Historical Records

Boundary	Workplace Related	Process Related
Internal	<ul><li>Workplace risk reviews, inspections and audits.</li><li>Workers compensation data</li><li>Historical records on incidents, accidents and near-miss events that are workplace related.</li><li>Health and environmental monitoring results</li><li>Enquiries/complaints received from employees</li></ul>	<ul><li>Process risk reviews, inspections and audits.</li><li>Historical records on equipment failure.</li><li>Historical records on incidents, accidents and near-miss events that are process related.</li><li>Spill reports</li><li>Process equipment</li></ul>

Boundary	Workplace Related	Process Related
		maintenance records • Information related to operational upsets
	• Training records • Injury/illness reports	
External	• Workplace risk reviews, inspections and audits by 3rd Parties	• Process risk reviews, inspections and audits by 3rd Parties
	• Findings of any prior Hazard Identification reviews. • Regulatory agency inspection reports. • Violations and monetary sanctions (fines, penalties, agency agreement orders, supplemental expenditures, lawsuits, settlements) • Enquiries/complaints received from the community and other external (interested) parties. • Other similar Organisation's risk reviews and performance.	

<u>Design or Engineering Documents</u>

Design or engineering documents are specific internal documents providing information related to location, equipment, physical and chemical properties etc.

The table below offers suggestions for potential sources (with some overlap) relative to workplace and process related hazards.

HIRA Information Sources for Design or Engineering Documents

Workplace Related	Process Related
• Specific task related working Instructions • Noise profiles and studies • Safe Systems of Work • Personal Protective Equipment	• Location and nature of the terrain and environmental conditions at the installation. • Chemical compatibility matrix for the chemicals present. • Process chemistry (if applicable), including any side or undesired reactions. • Materials of construction. • Power supply. • Pressure relief, depressurising, and flare data. • Process type/design and utility data, such as Process Flow Diagrams (PFD), Piping and Instrumentation Diagrams (P&ID), and Process Operating Envelopes. • Plans for construction, transportation, and installation activities. • Design philosophies, including manning, operating, maintenance, safety, shutdown, emergency and control. • Facility layout, including the location of major equipment and occupied

Workplace Related	Process Related
	buildings. • Description of neighbouring facilities, operations and areas of occupancy.

- Principal operations and other activities
- Chemical inventories and physical and chemical properties.
- Standard Operating Procedures
- Site hazard and Risk Register (we will cover Risk Registers in Element 4 - Actions Management)
- Emergency response plans.
- Chemical and equipment handling.

<u>Note:</u> There a number of expressions and terms used above that might be new to you. Don't worry about those, I just want to emphasise the various sources that are available.

The above lists are not extensive. It is intended as a starting point to expand based upon your Organisation's requirements.

Creating a detailed checklist of internal and external HIRA information sources will allow you and your Organisation to periodically review and update records.

E3.5 STEP 1: Hazard Identification

E3.5.1 Types of Hazards

You will recall that a hazard is defined as:

 Source with a potential to cause injury and ill health (I.e., a source with a consequence).

A wide range of hazard types exist as illustrated in the table below, with examples:

Types of Hazards

Type of Hazard	Example
Physical hazards	<ul><li>Wet floors</li><li>Loose electrical cables</li><li>Objects protruding in walkways or doorways</li></ul>
Ergonomic hazards	<ul><li>Lifting heavy objects</li><li>Stretching the body</li><li>Twisting the body</li><li>Poor desk seating</li></ul>
Psychological hazards	<ul><li>Heights</li><li>Loud sounds</li><li>Tunnels</li><li>Bright lights</li></ul>
Environmental hazards	<ul><li>Room temperature</li><li>Ventilation</li><li>Contaminated air</li><li>Photocopiers</li><li>Some office plants</li></ul>

Type of Hazard	Example
	• Acids
Hazardous substances	• Alkali • Solvents
Biological hazards	• Hepatitis B • New strain influenza
Radiation hazards	• Electric welding flashes Sunburn

E3.5.2 What's Our Hazard Focus?

Our focus is **workplace and process risks**. Hence, we will focus on **workplace and process hazards**.

Workplace and process hazards are both very different.

- Ignore workplace or process hazards at your Organisation's peril.

- Identifying workplace and process hazard is not an option or a luxury. It's an essential contributor towards successfully managing risks within your Organisation.

Workplace and process hazards have unique characteristics as shown in the table below:

Hazard Characteristics

Workplace Hazard Characteristics	Process Hazard Characteristics
• Tend to be physical hazards. • Easier to recognise. • Consequences are localised	• Less tangible and not easy to recognise. • Are a result of the inherent (I.e intrinsic) properties of the materials used, operating and handling conditions. • Widespread consequences and potentially catastrophic (I.e., with multiple loss of life).

The image below reflects the above points relative to consequence and likelihood.

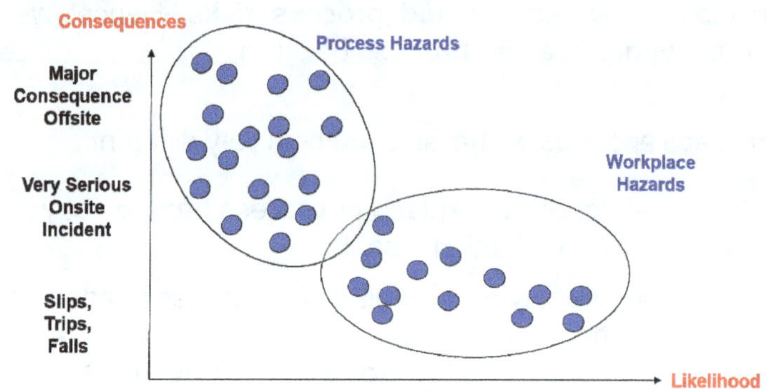

EXAMPLE

Examples of workplace and process hazards include:

Workplace Hazard Examples	Process Hazard Examples
• Slips, Trips and Falls	• Reactive explosions due to **chemicals** mixing
• Heat - burns	• Flammable explosions
• Cold - hypothermia	• Physical explosions due to sudden releases of material
• **Electrical** - shocks and short circuits	
• Impact - physical injury	• Toxic **chemical** releases.
• Noise - hearing impairment	
• Vibration hazards	• Fires (exposure to ignition sources such as **electrical**).
• **Mechanical** hazards - rotating equipment	
• **Chemical** - exposure.	• Corrosive **chemicals**
	• **Mechanical** failure related to stress/ fatigue

It can be seen from the table above that there is **potential for overlap** between workplace and process hazards, but each will result in unique consequences.

 Process hazards resulting in an unplanned or uncontrolled release of material from primary containment are more commonly known as "Loss of Primary Containment".

E3.5.3 Techniques for Hazard Identification

There are numerous HIRA methods available and this is most prevalent when it comes to **Hazard Identification** techniques.

Even offering a "short" overview of each method has the potential of making this book cumbersome and confusing. However, it can be useful to be aware of the more popular techniques, as shown in the table below.

Hazard Identification Techniques

Hazard Identification Technique	Details
HAZID Review (HAZard IDentification)	<ul><li>A technique for "**first level**" (or early) identification of potential workplace and process hazards.</li><li>Can be applied within projects, operations and other activities for identifying hazards through the various life cycles within an Organisation, including:<ul><li>Conceptual - designing (early) stage</li><li>Development - design available and operations decided.</li><li>Realisation - prior to commissioning.</li><li>Operational - or utilisation, prior to any changes</li><li>Improvement - prior to any operational enhancements and associated changes,</li><li>Decommissioning - prior to mothballing, cessation or disposal.</li></ul></li></ul>

Hazard Identification Technique	Details
HAZOP Review (HAZard and OPerability)	<ul><li>One of the more widely accepted and powerful of the hazard identification and assessment tools available for reviewing the process and operational aspects.</li><li>It is carried out in varying degrees of detail throughout a project after design checks have been completed.</li><li>HAZOP is not a design tool but a supplementary team checking exercise which also includes the operational aspect of a design.</li></ul>
Job Safety Analysis (JSA)	<ul><li>A standard term used widely to describe a hazard analysis tool used to breakdown a job into tasks, identify the safety hazards in each task and evaluate the control measures for each hazard.</li><li>Involves an individual or a small team at the work site or in the office.</li><li>Generally focuses on safety and does not cover service quality, health or environment.</li></ul>
Process Hazard Analysis (PHA)	<ul><li>A multi-disciplinary team uses brainstorming techniques to analyse hazards in a proposed or existing process, project or design.</li><li>Can be applied to any situation where an undesired event could occur, but it is generally applied to large projects or complex processes to ensure that all hazards have been analysed and</li></ul>

Hazard Identification Technique	Details
	that the control measures in place are adequate to ensure the risk level has been reduced to an acceptable level.
Task Hazard Analysis (THA)	• Task Hazard Analysis is a <u>PHA at the task level</u>. • Generally, a pre-job review conducted before commencement of the activity to ensure that all Hazards have been analysed and that the control measures in place are adequate to ensure the risk levels have been reduced to an acceptable level. • THAs always typically involve sub-contractors and even clients and third parties.
Quantified Risk Assessment (QRA)	• A highly specialised PHA using statistical data to quantify risks. • QRAs are typically performed by external consultants.

E3.5.4 Which HIRA Technique Should You Choose?

Before selecting your HIRA technique (for hazard identification **and/or** risk assessment), there are a number of factors regarding their characteristics that you should take into consideration.

These include ensuring that they are:

- Justifiable and appropriate to the situation or Organisation.

- Able to provide results in a form that enhances understanding of the nature of the risk and how it can be treated.

- Capable of being used in a manner that is traceable, repeatable and verifiable.

Let's assume you (or your Organisation) have not done any HIRA reviews or just done a few.

Referring back to our Table: Hazard Identification Techniques:
Our preferred option would be a HAZID review....because, it's a technique for **first level** (or early) identification of potential workplace and process hazards.

The HAZID technique would satisfy our characteristic requirements (I.e., justifiable and appropriate, provide results, enhances understanding, traceable, repeatable and verifiable etc).

Following the first level review and enhancing your understanding of the nature of risks, further decisions can be made on the need for a more detailed HIRA review using other techniques, if needed.

Every HIRA tool or technique offers a certain depth of analysis. Reviews going one layer down (I.e. as with a HAZID) might be adequate and cost-effective.

- Not every Organisation needs an in-depth, layer of analysis approach.

- Their size, resources, operations, maturity, experience etc may preclude them from using more sophisticated tools in the first place.

- Having supported several Organisations over a 30 year period and across a range of sectors, I have found HAZID's to be highly effective and worthwhile for **initial** HIRA reviews.

- Each HIRA technique allows you to peel away another layer.

By using the HAZID review technique, you are removing the outer layer (the first level). Depending on what you find, you might go a little deeper. However, the more layers you peel away, the greater the complexity, skill set requirement, quality and quantity of data, time for assessment, Organisation maturity etc.

The important point here is that you are in control over how many layers you want to remove and when you want to do a deeper analysis for supporting decisions.

For HAZID reviews, I could have just as easily replaced the word "**first**" with "**entry**" (I.e. "entry level" HIRA technique).

Perhaps you're familiar with the **Pareto principle** (also known as the **80/20** rule, the law of the vital few, or the **principle** of factor sparsity), which states that, for many events, roughly 80% of the results come from 20% of the effort.

HAZID reviews provide all the necessary foundations and groundwork to identify and help determine if you need to do a deeper analysis.

In conclusion:
- If you already have an enhanced understanding of risks, alternative methods, other than a HAZID, may be required to allow for that deeper dive and peeling away layers.
- Otherwise, a HAZID review would be a very good starting position.

E3.5.5 HAZID Review Technique

I have made reference to HAZID reviews a number of times now, especially in context to being a "**first level**" (or entry) method for Hazard Identification.

I want to provide you with an introduction to the HAZID review technique.

This section might get heavy? However, I must emphasise that it's only a basic overview as I want to keep it as light as possible.

- There are plenty of sources on the Internet detailing the mechanics of HAZIDs, and other HIRA methods.
- As with every HIRA method, it's advisable that the Organisation has people with the necessary skill set and experience in the application of the methods (see below - conducting HAZID reviews).

Before embarking on your HAZID review, it's important to make sure that you have the necessary tools.

HAZID reviews involve brainstorming and it will be a terrible waste of resources if you overlook planning and preparation, **especially your Organisation's resources.**

<u>**HAZID Review Essentials**</u>

The table below provides an overview of HAZID review essentials:

HAZID Review Essentials

Essentials	Details
Information sources for providing input data.	The 2 primary sources of information for a HAZID review are: ● Historical Records on incidents, accidents etc; and ● Design or Engineering Documents Refer back to the section titled "Information Sources for HIRA Reviews" for more details.
HAZID review enabling documents	● HIRA Procedure ● Risk Criteria ● Risk Assessment Criteria ● HAZID Terms of Reference (ToR) Document ● HAZID Procedure ● Checklists ● Recording Sheets *(Summary provided below)*

HAZID Review Enabling Documents

Enabling documentation for HAZID reviews varies amongst Organisations. The following can be considered as "typical" key enabling documents:

Typical HAZID Review Enabling Documents

Document	Summary of format and content
Terms of Reference (ToR) Document	A typical ToR will include: ● Objectives. ● Scope.

Document	Summary of format and content
	<ul><li>Planning and preparation requirements.</li><li>Type of hazards to be included.</li><li>Methodology, including parameters and deviations, to be used and whether risk ranking will be used.</li><li>Supporting documents.</li><li>Personnel that are required to attend the meeting.</li><li>Schedule and deliverables.</li><li>Report approver, recipient, and distribution list.</li><li>Reference documents (e.g., site layout, process type).</li></ul>
HAZID Procedure	In addition to the standard aspects within the procedure (I.e., definitions, abbreviations, reference documents etc), typical aspects include:<ul><li>Purpose</li><li>Scope & Intent</li><li>Introduction</li><li>Requirements for a HAZID ToR (see above)</li><li>Team Composition - Roles and Responsibilities</li><li>Methodology</li><li>Documenting, Reporting, Tracking and Follow Up Aspects</li></ul>
Checklists	The checklist covers a wide variety of workplace and process related hazards and not all the items in the checklist will be applicable, however, the process is systematic in approach to avoid oversight. The HAZID checklist includes details on:

Document	Summary of format and content
	<ul><li>Hazard type</li><li>Guide word to focus attention</li><li>Expanders to facilitate team discussions and brainstorming.</li></ul>
Recording Sheets	As the team discusses specific hazards using HAZID the guide words presented in the checklist, details are recorded in tabular format as record sheets.

HAZID Method Advantages and Disadvantages

Some of the advantages and disadvantages of a HAZID review includes:

HAZID Method Advantages and Disadvantages

Advantages	Disadvantages
<ul><li>Great "first level" (or early) tool for identification and assessment of workplace and process hazards.</li><li>Provides essential input to project development decisions.</li><li>Highly valuable as a cross-check review tool allowing guidance on the use of other HIRA techniques.</li></ul>	<ul><li>Tends to limit creative thinking. However, the HAZID Leader can influence to a certain extent.</li><li>Used alone, introduces the potential of limiting to already known hazards and no new hazard types are identified</li><li>On their own can limit the ability to satisfy regulatory requirements. However, this can be addressed with inclusion in checklists.</li></ul>

Conducting HAZID Reviews

Organisations may elect to have the HAZID review facilitated via an external party or consultant, however, this can be costly and prohibit smaller sized Organisations due to a lack of financial or other resources.

- In the first attempt, the "team" may not have extensive experience in the HAZID process.

- **Any HAZID review is a step improvement** I.e., people met, did a brainstorming exercise and identified potentials hazards and risks.

A typical example of what happens in a HAZID review is as follows:

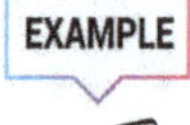

- For each hazard identified, the team reviews the consequence category and determines the product of consequence and likelihood (unmitigated I.e., using existing control measures).

- If the risk is unacceptable (relative to the Organisation's Risk Criteria), the team will focus on selecting additional control measures.

- The team reassesses the change in the risk level as a result of any mitigation (I.e., additional control measure).

- The intention is to reduce the risk level to meet the Organisation's Risk Criteria requirements for acceptability.

- Actions are recorded and assigned (use the **SMART** principle - **S**pecific, **M**easurable, **A**chievable, **R**elevant and **T**imely).

- During the HAZID brainstorming session, the team might identify a different, but more significant consequence (I.e., environmental, financial etc).

- This will then become the "motivating factor" for risk assessment.

- There will be an equivalent table, but using the factors for consequences in that "higher risk" category.

- Many Organisations combine all the consequence categories and have one table that they use in the HAZID process. This allows the team to have a greater range of creative thinking about the various consequences.

HAZID Review Method Summary

The table below provides a summary of the HAZID review method:

HAZID Review Method Summary

Feature	HAZID Method
Applicability	<ul><li>Workplace</li><li>Process</li><li>Application has widened in recent years including usage in software applications, medical devices, administrative procedures etc.</li></ul>
Purpose	<ul><li>Identify potential workplace and process hazards and associated consequences.</li><li>Support in the evaluation of risk based upon existing control measures (I.e.,</li></ul>

Feature	HAZID Method
	unmitigated). • Identify, apply additional control measures (if necessary) and determine risk reduction impact (I.e., mitigated). • Provide support to the Organisation and management in its efforts to manage risks.
Who does them?	• Experienced multi-discipline team, led (chaired) by experienced HAZID practitioners.
What's involved?	• A creative, structured and systematic approach that is focused and methodical.
How is it done?	• Use a checklist of potential workplace and process hazards to facilitate discussions.
When should it be done?	• Can be done at various life cycle stages of a process or project including conceptual, development, realisation, operation, improvement and decommissioning.

E3.5.6 Expectations from Hazard Identification Reviews

Applying whichever tool or technique (e.g., HAZID), hazards will be identified during the brainstorming session by the team.

Hazards that are identified will be fed into the Risk Assessment process to establish what's the potential risk exposure level.

<u>Relative to workplace and process hazards:</u>

The expectation from the Hazard Identification review is to identify potential workplace and process hazards and associated consequences. Having identified the hazard, the next step is to **assess the risk**?

E3.6 STEP 2: Risk Assessment

E3.6.1 What is Risk Assessment?

The objective of a risk assessment is to assess the hazards identified. In other words, it's the application of our Risk Equation:

Risk = [Consequence] * [Likelihood]
Risk = [Consequence] * [Likelihood] = [Hazard] * [Likelihood]

In order to support a "decision-driven" risk assessment process, an Organisation will need to have in place mechanisms that will:

1. **Transpose** the hazards identified into risks based upon the Risk Equation; and

2. Facilitate the **risk acceptance** decision process.

The 2 steps above are unique and we need to establish criteria and/or tools that support both mechanisms.

In the first instance, we need Risk Assessment Criteria that will allow us to transpose (I.e., transfer to a different context) hazards into risks.

E3.6.2 Transposing Hazards into Risks

The HIRA Team will identify hazards during the brainstorming session using checklists developed and endorsed by the Organisation.

The Organisation might have tables similar to the ones below for consequences (based on impacted areas) and likelihood.

Category Based Consequences

CONSEQUENCES			
People	Financial - Assets	Environmental Impact	Reputation
Slight health effect / injury	Slight damage	Slight effect	Slight impact
Minor health effect / injury	Minor damage	Minor effect	Limited impact
Major health effect / injury	Localised damage	Localised effect	Considerable impact
Permanent disability or 1 to 3 fatalities	Major damage	Major effect	National impact
Multiple fatalities	Extensive damage	Massive effect	International impact

Potential Likelihood

LIKELIHOOD	
Very Unlikely	Never heard of in the industry and/or from another similar Organisation
Unlikely	Have heard of it in the industry and/or from another similar Organisation
Possible	Has happened once in our Organisation since we began operations
Likely	Has happened several times in our Organisation since we began operations
Very Likely	Happens several times a year in our Organisation since we began operations

The format of both these tables can vary significantly between Organisations.

Micro and small Organisations may have scaled down versions, whereas large Organisations (with multiple sites and international locations) may have much more detail.

Our Risk Equation is:

Risk = [Consequence] * [Likelihood]

With the above 2 tables, we can now fulfil the requirements of our Risk Equation.

In fact, we can even merge both tables and have a combined table for workplace and process hazards, as shown below:

People Related Consequences and Potential Likelihood

LIKELIHOOD	People Related Consequences				
	Slight health effect / injury	Minor health effect / injury	Major health effect / injury	Permanent disability or 1 to 3 fatalities	Multiple fatalities
Very Unlikely	OK?	?	?	?	?
Unlikely	?	?	?	?	?
Possible	?	?	?	?	?
Likely	?	?	?	?	?
Very Likely	?	?	?	?	!

With the above table, **we have now transposed our hazards identified into risks.**

However, the table above has a lot of "**????**"

But, we do have a "gut feel" for some risks. For instance, **we don't want multiple fatalities being very likely!**

But:
- What about multiple fatalities being likely? Or
- How about multiple fatalities being possible?

Therein lies a conundrum - how do we decide whether the risk is acceptable or not?

How can the Organisation decide on accepting a risk?

E3.6.3 Developing Risk Assessment Criteria

We discussed **Risk Attitude** very early in Element 1.

Unfortunately, some authors forget completely to discuss Risk Attitude or they bury it so deep in their literature, that it loses its meaning and importance.

The Organisation's attitude plays a very important role in establishing their Risk Acceptance Criteria and we **must** take it into consideration.

Let's revisit our definitions:

<u>Risk Attitude is defined as</u>:
The Organisation's approach to assess and eventually pursue, retain, take or turn away from risk.

<u>Risk Criteria is defined as</u>:
Terms of reference against which the significance of a risk is evaluated.

Risk Criteria helps the Organisation make decisions on whether the risk is low enough or it will require attention to make it low enough to be acceptable (I.e., to pursue, retain, take or turn away from risk).

Readers will be aware that the word "**acceptable**" has spawned an entire science in context to behaviour, game-theory etc. This is <u>beyond the scope of this book.</u>

It's very important to get Risk Criteria requirements embedded at the beginning of your Organisation's risk management journey because it sets the foundation for Risk Attitude.

If an Organisation has a **risk-averse** attitude, it will favour criteria that exhibit a **positive bias** towards avoidance I.e., this is a **Risk Attitude-**

bias pairing.

The Risk Attitude-bias pairing is unique. It is a reflection of the motivation that the Organisation has relative to that risk.

I first introduced Risk Criteria when we discussed the importance of Risk Attitude and Motivators (See Element 1 - Risk Attitude).

Using an Organisation's Risk Attitude motivators, we can develop bespoke Risk Criteria.

The Organisation might choose to adopt a simple **traffic light approach** for their risk level acceptability criteria, as shown below:

Traffic Light Approach for Risk Level Acceptability Criteria

Risk Level	Acceptability Criteria	Description
High	Unacceptable	**Further control measures must be found** to reduce the risk to Medium or Low in order to proceed. If this is not feasible and the job (etc) still needs to proceed, the risk must be endorsed by the highest level/authority within the Organisation (I.e Risk Owners).
Medium	Acceptable	**Further control measures need to be investigated**. The job (etc) can still proceed if these further control measures are rejected on a cost-benefit basis, however, the risk must be endorsed senior level management with responsibility delegation from the Risk Owner(s).
Low	Negligible	**No further control measures**

Risk Level	Acceptability Criteria	Description
		required. Should be verified that procedures or controls are, or will be, in place.

This simple traffic light approach will provide the Organisation criteria and guidance on risk acceptability.

- Organisations evolve over time in a number of different aspects (e.g., size, nature of operations, locations, headcount etc).

- It's important that an Organisation's Risk Criteria and acceptability is periodically reviewed to ensure that it's fit for purpose and that it is a true reflection of the Organisation's risk appetite.

But, how does the Organisation apply acceptability criteria to risks identified?

E3.6.4 Developing a Risk Assessment Matrix

Having developed a simple traffic light approach, we now need to apply the acceptability criteria to the risks identified....**but how?**

In an earlier section, we looked at transposing hazards into risks and created the table below:

People related consequences and potential likelihood

LIKELIHOOD	People Related Consequences				
	Slight health effect / injury	Minor health effect / injury	Major health effect / injury	Permanent disability or 1 to 3 fatalities	Multiple fatalities
Very Unlikely	OK?	?	?	?	?
Unlikely	?	?	?	?	?
Possible	?	?	?	?	?
Likely	?	?	?	?	?
Very Likely	?	?	?	?	!

You might recall our conundrum? How do we decide whether the risk is acceptable or not?

The table above has a lack of clarity with the "**???**"

Using traffic light colours, we now have our Risk Level Acceptability Criteria table as follows:

Traffic Light Approach for Risk Level Acceptability Criteria

Risk Level	Acceptability Criteria	Description
High	Unacceptable	**Further control measures must be found** to reduce the risk to Medium or Low in order to proceed. If this is not feasible and the job (etc) still needs to proceed, the risk must be endorsed by the highest level/authority within the Organisation (I.e Risk Owners).
Medium	Acceptable	**Further control measures need to be investigated**. The job (etc) can still proceed if these further control measures are rejected on a cost-benefit basis, however, the risk must be endorsed senior level management with responsibility delegation from the risk owner(s).
Low	Negligible	**No further control measures required**. Should be verified that procedures or controls are, or will be, in place.

We are now well positioned to add colour to our "black and white" likelihood-consequence table, as given below:

Colourful Risk Assessment Matrix

LIKELIHOOD	People Related Consequences				
	Slight health effect / injury	Minor health effect / injury	Major health effect / injury	Permanent disability or 1 to 3 fatalities	Multiple fatalities
Very Unlikely	Low	Low	Low	Low	Low
Unlikely	Low	Low	Low	Medium	Medium
Possible	Low	Low	Medium	Medium	High
Likely	Low	Medium	Medium	High	High
Very Likely	Medium	Medium	High	High	High

The Organisation has developed their very own **colourful Risk Assessment Matrix.**

The Organisation has "colour vision" and can now see risks in colour.

Are there any limitations to the colourful Risk Assessment Matrix?

E3.6.5 Colourful Risk Assessment Matrix Limitations

By applying acceptability criteria and embedding requirements into a matrix format, the Organisation developed its **Colourful Risk Assessment Matrix**, as shown below:

Colourful Risk Assessment Matrix

LIKELIHOOD	People Related Consequences				
	Slight health effect / injury	Minor health effect / injury	Major health effect / injury	Permanent disability or 1 to 3 fatalities	Multiple fatalities
Very Unlikely	Low	Low	Low	Low	Low
Unlikely	Low	Low	Low	Medium	Medium
Possible	Low	Low	Medium	Medium	High
Likely	Low	Medium	Medium	High	High
Very Likely	Medium	Medium	High	High	High

- Similar tables can be developed for the other consequence categories (I.e., Financial, Environmental etc), if necessary.

- A collection is referred to as "**Risk Assessment Matrices**".

There are many Risk Assessment Matrices that have been developed and published. However, their development and application present unique challenges. An effective Risk Assessment Matrix should take the following into consideration:

- Be simple to use and understand.
- Doesn't require extensive knowledge of quantitative risk analysis to use.
- Has clear guidance on applicability relative to the consequence category.
- Has consistent likelihood ranges that cover the full spectrum of potential consequences.
- Has clearly defined acceptable and unacceptable risk levels.

Whilst we have provided a means for distinguishing risk level based on traffic light colours, **what happens if there are hundreds of reds?**

The challenge then for the Organisation is in determining the criticality of risks (I.e., **which risk is redder**).

Can we improve on this colourful approach?

Perhaps, we can assess risks quantitatively without getting too deep and complex?

E3.6.6 The Quantitative Risk Assessment Matrix

Having identified hazards and assessed them for risks using the **Colourful Risk Assessment Matrix**, we will end up with several risks with their colourful significance (e.g., Red, Yellow or Green).

It is inevitable that with such a small colour palette, we will have many risks that are Red. This is not an ideal situation because it will affect judgement and overall decision.

Having hundreds or thousands of risks to manage with equal priority will potentially make the risk management process ineffective and meaningless (e.g., all "red" risks become equal).

Add to the above cocktail of colour that Red risks will involve the Risk Owner's intervention, you then add administrative burden and further delay in addressing risks that can be potentially supercritical.

There is a solution….

As you look through your list of risks, you start to notice that even though they are red, some risks are actually redder (I.e., more critical).

Let's revisit our **Colourful Risk Assessment Matrix** and assign a scale for both Likelihood and Consequence, ranging from "0" to "5".

Our Risk Equation is:

Risk = [Consequence] * [Likelihood]

Therefore, by applying our Risk Equation, we can create the following table:

Quantified Risk Assessment Matrix with Colour

LIKELIHOOD	People Related Consequences				
	Slight health effect / injury (1)	Minor health effect / injury (2)	Major health effect / injury (3)	Permanent disability or 1 to 3 fatalities (4)	Multiple fatalities (5)
Very Unlikely (1)	Low = 1	Low = 2	Low = 3	Low = 4	Low = 5
Unlikely (2)	Low = 2	Low = 4	Low = 6	Medium = 8	Medium = 10
Possible (3)	Low = 3	Low = 6	Medium = 9	Medium = 12	High = 15
Likely (4)	Low = 4	Medium = 8	Medium = 12	High = 16	High = 20
Very Likely (5)	Medium = 5	Medium = 10	High = 15	High = 20	High = 25

We have now added another layer of granularity to our colourful Risk Assessment Matrix with numbers.

<u>For example</u>:
Red = 25 **is redder than** Red = 20

There is now a choice of using either Colour or a Quantitative Risk Assessment Matrix…perhaps both?

But, can we add even more granularity?

E3.6.7 How to Fine Tune Your Risk Assessment Matrix

Having a Risk Assessment Matrix that is not only colourful but offers additional clarity with numbers is a great step forward in facilitating and justifying decisions.

Periodically, the Organisation might take a step back, review and modify or expand their acceptability criteria and subsequently their Risk Assessment Matrix.

This "fine tuning" is important because it allows the Organisation to ensure the assessment of risks is aligned with its Risk Attitude.

Perhaps, the Organisation might have become more risk averse?

There are specific ways in which an Organisation can fine tune their Risk Assessment Matrix.

<u>For example</u>:
Having revisited the **Likelihood table**, the Organisation might conclude that there is limited scope for clarification I.e., it's at optimum.

Potential Likelihood

LIKELIHOOD	
Very Unlikely	Never heard of in the industry and/or from another similar Organisation
Unlikely	Have heard of it in the industry and/or from another similar Organisation
Possible	Has happened once in our Organisation since we began operations
Likely	Has happened several times in our Organisation since we began operations
Very Likely	Happens several times a year in our Organisation since we began operations

But for People related consequences, the Organisation might decide that the original table can be enhanced with additional guidance. It could include some guidance notes as follows:

Enhanced People related consequences category with guidance notes

CONSEQUENCES	
People Related Consequence	**Guidance Notes**
Slight health effect / injury	• Not affecting work performance or causing disability. • Agents which are not hazardous to health. • Not detrimental to individual employability or to the performance of present work.
Minor health effect / injury	• Affecting work performance, such as restriction to activities (Restricted Work Case) or a need to take a few calendar days to recover fully • Agents which have limited health effects which are reversible, e.g., irritants, many food poisoning bacteria. • Detrimental to the performance of present work, such as the curtailment of activities or some calendar days to recover fully, maximum one week.
Major health effect / injury	• Resulting in permanent partial disability or affecting work performance in the longer term, such as prolonged absence from work • Agents which are capable of irreversible damage without serious disability, e.g., noise, poorly designed

CONSEQUENCES	
People Related Consequence	**Guidance Notes**
	manual handling tasks • Leading to permanent partial disablement or unfitness for work or detrimental to the performance of work over an extended period, such as long term absence.
Permanent disability or 1 to 3 fatalities	• Agents which are capable of irreversible damage with serious disability or death, e.g., corrosives, known human carcinogens • Alternatively victim with permanent total disablement or unfitness for work. Also includes the possibility of multiple fatalities (maximum 3) in close succession due to the incident, e.g., explosion
Multiple fatalities	• Agents with potential to cause multiple fatalities, e.g., chemicals with acute toxic effects (e.g., hydrogen sulphide, carbon monoxide), known human carcinogens. • May include four fatalities in close succession due to the incident, or multiple fatalities (four or more) each at different points and/or with different activities

- Adding more detail and clarity will facilitate the fine-tuning process.
- The HIRA team are able to make more informed decisions regarding the risk.

- It's that "**sniper**" approach again!

There are (of course) no bounds on creativity.

<u>For example</u>:
Increasing the colour palette by adding more colours (e.g., Orange).

- Whatever "tweaks" you do, they have to be aligned with the requirements of your Organisation's Risk Attitude and Risk Criteria.

- The ongoing development of an Organisation's Risk Assessment Matrix is an iterative process.

- The emphasis here (again) is on the importance of periodic reviews in that it must never be overlooked nor undervalued.

E3.6.8 Which Risk Assessment Matrix Should You Use?

The combinations and permutations for **Risk Assessment Matrices** are numerous and can be very confusing during HIRA reviews.

- Depending on the amount of granularity required, some Organisation's keep their Risk Assessment Matrices simple, but highly effective (I.e. colourful).
- Some Organisations go for a quantitative approach and make it even more complex by increasing options.

In our **Quantified and Colourful Risk Assessment Matrix,** we had a scale for consequence and likelihood based on a **5 by 5** grid (denoted as 5 x 5).

Quantified Risk Assessment Matrix with Colour

LIKELIHOOD	People Related Consequences				
	Slight health effect / injury (1)	Minor health effect / injury (2)	Major health effect / injury (3)	Permanent disability or 1 to 3 fatalities (4)	Multiple fatalities (5)
Very Unlikely (1)	Low = 1	Low = 2	Low = 3	Low = 4	Low= 5
Unlikely (2)	Low = 2	Low = 4	Low = 6	Medium = 8	Medium = 10
Possible (3)	Low = 3	Low = 6	Medium = 9	Medium = 12	High = 15
Likely (4)	Low = 4	Medium =8	Medium = 12	High = 16	High = 20
Very Likely (5)	Medium = 5	Medium = 10	High = 15	High = 20	High = 25

My own experienced, based upon hundreds of HIRA reviews, has shown that this combination (**5 x 5**) is the optimum for facilitating discussions and provide direction during brainstorming sessions…..keep it simple.

However, Risk Assessment Matrices can vary significantly between Organisations. They can be **(3 x 3), (4 x 4), (8 x 8)** and so on. It's even possible to have several bands for likelihood and less for consequences giving matrices that can be **(2 x 3), (3 x 9)** etc.

- The bigger the Risk Assessment Matrix, the greater the ranges for consequence and likelihood and the greater the confusion, discussion, debate and subjectivity.

- There is always a trade-off between quality and quantity.

Organisations evolve over time and keeping the same assessments and criteria can create liability issues and give a false sense of security.

For continuity and stability, it's important that the Organisation periodically reviews their HIRA Procedure and Risk Assessment Matrix. This will not only ensure that it is fit for purpose but that it also reflects the Organisation's risk appetite and criteria.

<u>For example</u>:
For large Organisations, there are potentially more risks and the (3 x 3) Risk Assessment Matrix that they having been using since inception might not be relevant anymore).

Provided there are periodic reviews to ensure alignment with the Organisation's Risk Criteria, keeping your Risk Assessment Matrix simple is the key to success.

Having identified our hazards and identified them, we now have a lot of actions. These actions will indicate what treatment will be required to meet acceptability.   But we need a plan…a Risk Treatment Plan.

E3.6.9 Developing Your Risk Treatment Plan

The Risk Treatment Plan is defined as a documented approach detailing:

How the chosen treatment options will be implemented.

Once you have completed your HIRA with your SMART Actions, it's time to formally document the output. The Risk Treatment Plan documents how risk control measures are going to be implemented.

Risk Treatment Plans don't have to be complex and they typically include the following components:

Risk Treatment Plan Components

	Treatment options	Reasons for selection, including expected benefits to be gained
	Accountability	For approving the treatment plan
	Responsibility	For implementing the treatment plan
	Actions	For treating the risk identified and assessed
	Resources	Requirements, including contingencies
	Measurement	Key Performance Indicators
	Monitoring	Reporting and monitoring requirements
	Timing / Schedules	For action implementation, reviews etc

- The Risk Treatment Plan can be integrated within an Organisation's Actions Management framework.

- The Risk Treatment Plan provides Risk Owners assurance that risks have been addressed, control measures established and resources allocated to manage the risks appropriately.

4.6 ELEMENT 4: Actions Management

E4.1 Criticality of Actions

Within any Risk Management Framework, actions are going to be generated as a result of reviews and assessments.

 In fact, the bulk of actions is most likely to be generated from HIRA reviews.

Regardless of where or how they originated, those actions will require prioritisation and responsible individuals appointed to ensure follow up and closure.

 Albeit Risk Owners will have been defined by the Organisation, it's equally important to ensure delegation of responsibility is clear if risk treatment actions have been assigned to specific individuals.

Delegated individuals must have the necessary support and resources otherwise actions will stagnate, not get closed out and potentially expose the Organisation to those risks.

Organisations can elect to categorise their risks relative to the impact on business continuity.

 For example:
During the risk assessment process, we had the following categories in our consequences matrix.

Category Based Consequences

CONSEQUENCES			
People	**Financial - Assets**	**Environmental Impact**	**Reputation**
Slight health	Slight	Slight effect	Slight impact

CONSEQUENCES			
effect / injury	damage		
Minor health effect / injury	Minor damage	Minor effect	Limited impact
Major health effect / injury	Localised damage	Localised effect	Considerable impact
Permanent disability or 1 to 3 fatalities	Major damage	Major effect	National impact
Multiple fatalities	Extensive damage	Massive effect	International impact

Even though we identified the impacted area and did some fine tuning with colours, numbers etc., we might still be left with asking the question "which risks are more important?"

When we take a closer look at our "category labelled risk portfolio", we start to see risks that:

- Significantly impact **Business**.

- Significantly impact **Operations**, more than Business.

- Are more **General**. Still important, but with a lesser impact on Operations and the Business.

Using this weighted or biased approach, the Organisation can have an alternative view on which risk it wants to prioritise I.e., the business impact is more severe than operations impact.

Of course, Organisations recognise that managing all risks are important and **some "risks are redder"**.

But, some redder risks are much more important because they could be out of business if the risk is realised. **These risks are business critical and can affect business continuity**.

- Readers, please take note that **Business Continuity** as a subject is large, complex and beyond the scope of this book.

- I have used the term here in context to reduced capability to operate its business functions as a result of a risk being realised.

By taking this weighted or biased approach, the Organisation can deal with actions in neatly labelled packages. It allows the Organisation to create a **Risk Register** relative to that label and criticality (I.e., Business, Operations etc).

By creating such Risk Registers, we have also increased the profile and visibility of Risk Treatment Plans.

For example:
With one glance, a Risk Owner can look at the **Business Risk Register** and make decisions on re-prioritisation, resource re-allocation etc...

E4.2 What's Are Risk Registers?

By filtering risks and placing them in uniquely labelled packages, we have increased the profile and visibility of Risk Treatment Plans.

Previously, we recognised a pattern when we looked at risk criticality, as follows:

- Significantly impact **Business**.

- Significantly impact **Operations**, more than Business.

- Are more **General**. Still important, but with a lesser impact on Operations and the Business.

Based on the above, we can create 3 distinct Risk Registers, as follows:

1. Business Risk Register
2. Operations Risk Register
3. General Risk Register - these can have several variations and can be location specific, workplace or and process risks specific etc

In fact, there are no restrictions on the number of Risk Registers or categories that an Organisation can have. They are bespoke.

However:-

- Risk Registers are unique.

- The larger the Organisation, the bigger the Risk Register and the greater the complexity.

- Having too many Risk Registers will dilute focus, increase confusion and weaken the Risk Management Framework.

Populating a Risk Register is fairly straightforward and involves 2 key steps:

1. **Filter** - review all risks in your risk portfolio and decide if the risk will impact the Business, Operations or are just General in nature.

2. **Resolve conflicts** - if there is an overlap, assign the risk a higher impact level.

<u>For example</u>:
Let's say the risk was borderline Operations/Business, I would opt to place the risk in the higher category. I can always downgrade later.

At a later stage, you can always downgrade the risk label and/or criticality, especially as more information becomes available.

The 2 step approach places risks, associated actions and treatment plans in their respective Risk Register. Taking this approach, we will also start to see a pattern.

With Risk Registers, the "normal" pattern (or trend) is an increase in the number of risks as you go down in criticality, as shown in the example below.

<u>For example</u>:
If an Organisation has 300 risks, they might have a distribution as follows:
- Business Risks = 25
- Operations Risks = 75
- General Risks = 200

Assuming the sifting process was done properly, let's suppose <u>for the same actions</u>, the distribution a year later was as follows:

<u>For example</u>:
A year later, the 300 risks are now distributed as follows:

- Business Risks = 70 (**+45**)
- Operations Risks = 130 (**+55**)
- General Risks = 100 (**-100**)

How would you react?

I suspect that if you are the Risk Owner, **you're not going to be very pleased**!

- Risk Registers not only allow additional granularity, but they can also show the "direction of travel".

- The Organisation can use these "direction" signals for focusing their efforts (e.g., poor leadership, commitment etc).

- When used effectively, Risk Registers are excellent performance indicators within the Risk Management Framework (which we will cover in **Element 5 - Performance Improvement**).

- The cautionary note here is "acknowledge the signal, but remember to avoid immediate judgement", because additional information might change the landscape.

<u>Remember</u>:
Garbage In = Garbage Out

E4.3 Format for Risk Registers

There are no specific requirements for the format of Risk Registers.

The golden rule is "it has to work functionally for your Organisation.

Regardless of format, Risk Register content can be summarised and presented as a Key Performance Indicator (KPI) - which we will cover in **Element 5 - Performance Improvement.**

In its simplest form, the Risk Register may contain:

- Risk Description;

- Risk Category (I.e., consequence or impact category);

- Risk Level (I.e., based on the risk assessment matrix is it red, yellow, green etc)

- Risk Register Category (I.e., Business, Operations etc);

- Risk Owner;

- Action required;

- Action by (I.e., responsible party);

- Due date; and

- Status.

The above template can, of course, be expanded or reduced.

<u>For example</u>:
If this register is specific to Business Risk then Item 3 can be removed....we know the register's

label.

For Risk Register format:

- Keep it simple.
- You can always add the "bells and whistles" later.
- The primary focus is to ensure risk management is travelling in the right direction for the Organisation.

Periodically, risk actions will need to be reviewed and changes made, specifically re-prioritisation of risks.

E4.4 Re-prioritising Risk Actions

Risk prioritisation is about addressing risks that impact the Organisation by taking into consideration:

1. Consequences and Likelihood

2. Importance relative to Business and Operations.

3. Accountability, availability and allocation of resources.

During HIRA reviews, the team will have assigned specific due dates.

Unless it's schedule specific, setting a due date is the team's first attempt at setting a priority for the risk action. The team will have made their decision on due dates relative to the Organisation's Risk Assessment Matrix (I.e., impact, criteria, acceptability etc).

However, selected dates may not "always" be correct. There might be a need for re-prioritisation.

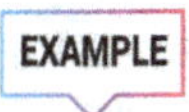

<u>For example</u>:
Let's assume that all the risk actions have now been filtered and we have created our Risk Registers using the format below:

- Risk Description;

- Risk Category (I.e., consequence or impact category);

- Risk Level (I.e., based on the risk assessment matrix is it red, yellow, green etc)

- Risk Register Category (I.e., Business,

Operations etc);

- Risk Owner;
- Action required;
- Action by (I.e., responsible party);
- Due date; and
- Status.

Our distribution of 300 risk actions are as follows:
- Business Risk Register = 25 risk actions
- Operations Risk Register = 75 risk actions
- General Risk Register = 200 risk actions.

When the Risk Owner reviews the above list of actions in the Business Risk Register, it's highly likely that they might have a different view on priority, especially as they have a wider picture on the overall business objectives, mission etc.

Priorities can change as a result of more information, especially related to business direction, operational needs etc.

Re-prioritisation of risks in Risk Registers, especially the Operations Risk Register, is quite common.

However, if there are significant differences between dates proposed by the HIRA team and re-prioritised dates, **this might indicate a flaw or clarity issues in the Risk Assessment Criteria** I.e., misalignment between the Risk Owners expectations and the HIRA team's interpretation of Risk Criteria.

If there are significant differences between the original and re-prioritised dates, this is a strong signal to review the risk assessment matrix, criteria etc.

Albeit not very popular for workplace and process related risk management, Organisations can elect to show risks as **Key Risk Indicators (KRI)** in their Risk Registers. This is almost equivalent to colour grading our colourful risks.

125

E4.5 Key Risk Indicators (KRI)

Depending on the Organisation and nature of activities, Organisations may elect to review risks via **Key Risk Indicators (KRI)**.

The OECD[4] defines **KRI** as:

An indicator that estimates the potential for some form of resource degradation using mathematical formula or models.

It is simpler to consider **KRI** as a measure used in management to indicate how risky an activity is.

Relative to workplace and process related risks, KRI is not commonly used.

However, there is no reason why an Organisation cannot use **KRI**, especially if they want to include them in their Risk Registers.

Relative to risk levels (I.e., based upon the Risk Assessment Matrix), KRI will provide an additional layer granularity within Risk Registers, thereby providing pointers for any subsequent re-prioritisation.

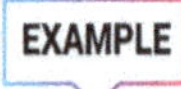

For example:

- Suppose the Organisation had 20 risks in their Business Register and each risk had a numerical value, which would represent the **KRI**.

- After closer examination, the Risk Owner might decide that KRI #20 is more significant because they have a new project in the pipeline that the HIRA team did not know about.

- The Risk Owner will re-prioritise the risk, most likely in consultation with the HIRA team and leader.

- Generally speaking, it is not normal for risks to be re-prioritised after HIRA reviews.

- If this happens frequently, there are significant issues that need to be addressed.

Key Risk Indicators (KRI) are not commonly used for workplace and process related risks. The tendency is to use Key Performance Indicators (KPI) and we will cover Key Performance Indicators (KPI) in our next Element.

4.7 ELEMENT 5: Performance Improvement

E5.1 What are Measure, Metric and KPI?

When it comes to measuring performance, **Measure, Metric and Key Performance Indicators (KPI)** are commonly used terms. However, they are often used interchangeably and often mistakenly interpreted.

The fundamental difference between Measure, Metric and Key Performance Indicator (KPI) is provided in the table below:

Fundamental Difference Between Measure, Metric and KPI

Term	Definition
Measure	• Is a fundamental, unit-specific term and tend to be number or value driven.
Metric	• A more appropriate term for highly standardised measurements based on procedures, calculation methods and systems for generating a number. • Metrics can be derived from one or more measures and tend to be goal or performance orientated.
Key Performance Indicator (KPI)	• Measurable value showing how effectively an Organisation is achieving or progressing their defined objectives. • KPIs are context-driven in that they can be driven by the Organisation's strategy and Risk Owners. • Values can be compared against past performance data or benchmarked against other similar Organisations.

Consider the following example:

You have a website and you plan to:
- **Measure** the website traffic.
- Monitor website traffic compared to a traffic goal as your **Metric**.
- Monitor that same site traffic but only look at content downloads as your **KPI**.

This simple example shows how Metrics take a broad approach, whereas KPI does a deeper dive.

In other words, Metrics cover the entire range, but KPI drill down deeper for comparative analysis.

This doesn't mean that Measures are not important. Both Metrics and KPI depend on measurement for their foundation.

To quote Peter Drucker: **"You can't manage what you can't measure".**

Of course, it is also reasonable to argue that "**you don't always need to measure to manage**".

Consider the following examples:

- I know when my hair needs cutting – I don't need a ruler;
- I know when my car windows need cleaning – I don't need a light meter; and
- I see that that the queue is long at the bus stop – I don't need a measuring tape for that.

E5.2 What Can You Measure?

As I mentioned previously:

Both Metrics and Key Performance Indicators (KPI) depend on measurement for their foundation.

For measurements that provide input on performance, they have to be:
1. Objective and specific
2. Serve a purpose relative to the Organisation's goals, objectives, targets, aspirations etc.
3. Easy to measure, collect and record
4. Accurate, current and easy to validate
5. Relatively easy to explain.

Let's review the above measurement characteristics relative to risk management - are they essential?

The Role of Measurement for Risk Management

Measurement Trait	Requirement relative to risk management
Objective and specific	**Yes** - workplace and process risks related
Serve a purpose	**Yes** - reviewing workplace and process risks management
Easy to measure, collect and record	**Yes** - associated with safety, hazards, incidents etc..there is substance.
Accurate, current and easy to validate	**Yes** - legal and other requirements (e.g., insurance).
Relatively easy to explain.	**Yes** - relates to hazards (I.e., cause harm).

We can expand the above list, if necessary. But, for now, we can conclude that there are specific aspects for focus in risk management regarding measurement (I.e., we are not going to waste our precious time and valuable resources).

With measurement, our purpose is to verify the effectiveness of "**workplace and process risk management**". To achieve this, we need to decide what we are going to Measure.

We know that:

Risk Management Framework = Foundations + Arrangements… or

Risk Management Framework = Risk Management Policy + Risk Management Plan

We have some guidance looking at the above requirements (I.e., safety, hazards, incidents etc), but we need to look further and deeper. Therefore, we could consider the following as potential opportunities for measurement:

Measurement Opportunities for Risk Management

Framework	Potential Opportunity for Measurement
Policy	• Development of the policy • Implementation of the policy • Effectiveness of the policy • Deviation from policy
Attitude	• Organisation's and individual manager's performance.
Control	• Developing details on nature and types of causes and consequences • Number of higher risks identified without management approval

Framework	Potential Opportunity for Measurement
HIRA	<ul><li>Effectiveness of risk treatment measures.</li><li>Critical equipment and procedures evaluated in a structured format utilising the risk assessment process</li><li>The number of operating procedures developed and documented, relative to the plan.</li><li>The number of risks assessments not conducted with personnel trained in techniques</li><li>The number of risk assessments, relative to the plan.</li></ul>
Actions Management	<ul><li>Progress in implementing risk treatment by reviewing the Risk Register.</li><li>Number of outstanding risk actions in the Risk Registers</li></ul>
Performance Improvement	<ul><li>Risk management performance against indicators</li></ul>
Reviewing	<ul><li>Continuous improvement in risk management</li><li>Deviation from the risk management plan</li><li>Number of accidents, incidents and near misses attributable to lack of or improper risk assessment</li></ul>

- Some of the measurements above could be just applied across many Elements (e.g., number of actions related to risk assessments).

- With measurement, there is potential to double, triple count etc.

- Measurement, Metrics and KPI provide a fertile ground for creativity, not only in selection but also in how they can be benchmarked and communicated within an Organisation.

Regardless of whichever measurement is selected, the Organisation will have to set out bespoke Metrics that can be used for reviewing performance otherwise it serves no purpose (I.e., it's just a collection of data).

- To avoid or minimise procrastination, Organisation's may wish to look at other similar entities. This will provide the added benefit of benchmarking.

- When it comes to selecting what to Measure, **remember that the intention is to serve a purpose**....it has to be functional.

Having decided on what we are going to Measure, we now have an opportunity to not only look at current status but also backwards and forwards (I.e., Leading and Lagging indicators).

E5.3 Introducing Leading and Lagging Indicators

At this stage, for measuring, the Organisation has now:

- Committed to measuring plus allocated resources;
- Selected relevant Metrics that it will periodically monitor and Measure; and
- Progressed with measuring "something"…!

Let's fast forward…the Organisation has accumulated a lot of data, verified accuracy etc.

What next?

Collected data offers the Organisation 3 unique vantage points or indicators. These include:

1. **Historical indicators** - change in specific measurements over time;

2. **Current indicators** - what are the measured values right now; and

3. **Future indicators** - predictive analysis based upon various factors that could be applied to the past and/or current measured values (e.g., design, operational, engineering changes etc).

Used in the above context, indicators are known as:

Lagging indicators	Looking backwards at historical performance and hence focus on outcomes.
Leading indicators	Looking forward offering a glimpse into future performance.

The Organisation can use these Leading and Lagging indicators to review their "solo-performance" or they can use them comparatively with similar Organisations (I.e., benchmarking).

- Of course, Lagging indicators are easy to Measure and Leading indicators are more difficult.

- Leading indicators are highly prone to subjectivity and error due to the quality of data.

For any Leading or Lagging indicator to be useful, they should:

- Clearly, indicate small changes in performance.

- Measure positive or negative aspects (i.e., what people are doing or failing to do).

- Facilitate feedback to all stakeholders (internal and external).

- Be reliable, credible and predictive to an extent.

- Focus dialogue and increase constructive problem solving around risk management.

- Provide transparency on what needs to be done for performance improvement.

- Track impact versus intention

- Just like measurement, there are thousands of indicators to choose from and the possibilities can be overwhelming.

- Organisations will need to be very specific as to which indicator is a **Key Performance Indicator (KPI)** I.e., measurable value that shows how effectively the Organisation is achieving their defined objectives, projects, programs, products or other initiatives.

To conclude:

Key Performance Indicators (KPI) help you understand how your Organisation is performing and Leading and Lagging Indicators provide the input for assessment.

E5.4 Developing Your Key Performance Indicators (KPI)

In Element 4 (Actions Management), I provided an introduction to **Key Risk Indicators (KRI)** and mentioned that **Key Performance Indicator (KPI)** is different.

You may recall that:

- KRI provides an overview of risks relative to their significance.

- KPI provides an overview of how effectively an Organisation is achieving its defined objectives, projects, programs, products or other initiatives.

There is no doubt that Key Performance Indicators (KPIs) play an important role and selecting the right KPI is largely driven by what the Organisation considers as important, hence they are unique to the Organisation.

But, they're all important....so which ones do I select....I hear you say...?

The simple answer is "the ones that matter to you and your Organisation". Perhaps not the response you were expecting?

Take the example below:

- If you are in Operations, you may have a specific focus on workplace risks

- If you are in Engineering, your focus is likely to be on process risks.

Whichever KPI grabs your attention, the architecture for successful Key Performance Indicators (KPI) has to be **SMART**.

The **SMART** acronym comprises of:

Specific	It should be clear what is being measured, they are understandable, easy to communicate and explain to others within your Organisation.
Measurable	They are meaningful in that they are not just qualitative, but quantitative and possibly measurable against set standards.
Achievable	They are easy to monitor, maintain and target a realistic/achievable goal
Relevant	It should offer insight into overall risk management/ performance.
Timely	Should follow a set time-frame I.e., annual, weekly etc.

Using **SMART**, let's apply the **6Ws** and develop our KPI as follows:

SMART Questions for KPI Development

	Why?	• Are we in a good spot? If "yes", why are we where we are? • Are we getting better or worse over time? If "yes", why are we where we are?
	What?	• Are we doing the right things consistently? • Is an effective Risk Management Framework in place across all parts of the Organisation (deployment)? • Is our Risk Management Framework proportionate to our hazards and risks?
	When?	• Are we measuring at the right times?
	Where?	• Where are we now relative to our

		overall risk management objectives?
		• Where are we now in terms of controlling our risks?
	Who?	• Are we doing the right things when it comes to managing the Organisation's risks?
		• Does our culture support our Risk Management Plan, particularly in the face of competing demands?
		• Is our risk management efficient?
	Ho**W**?	• How do we compare with others?

Reduce or expand the above questions, as appropriate for your Organisation.

 Applying **SMART** with Why, What, When etc., will build a more detailed picture for what the Organisation requires (I.e., **W**hy **S**pecific, **W**hy **M**easurable, **W**hy **A**chievable, **W**hy **R**elevant, **W**hy **T**imely etc).

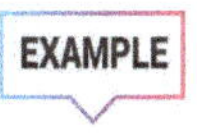 Given below are some typical examples of KPI across a range of areas. We will cover risk management specifically in the next section.

Safety Metrics	**Financial Metrics**
• Reported Accidents/Incidents	• Profit
• Reporting Near Misses	• Production Costs.
• Safety Audits and Inspections	• Selling Cost
• Corrective Actions	• Sales
• Employee Training	• EBITDA (Earnings Before Interest, Taxes, Depreciation, & Amortisation)
• Spend	

Customer Metrics	HR (People) Metrics
• Customer Lifetime Value (CLV)	• Employee Turnover Rate (ETR)
• Customer Acquisition Cost (CAC)	• Percentage Of Response To Open Positions
• Customer Satisfaction & Retention	• Employee Satisfaction
• Number Of Customers	

Developing and selecting KPI for your Organisation is an important step towards achieving performance improvement.

E5.5 Selecting Leading and Lagging KPI

For the Organisation's Risk Management Framework, selected KPI should reveal the effectiveness of the framework relative to the historical position and future objectives. Hence, **KPI** has to be a combination of **Leading** and **Lagging** indicators.

Research is the initial effort required when you are trying to establish KPI for risk management because chances are high that someone has already:

- In a similar Organisation has done the hard work for you in defining KPI.

- Got quantitative KPI data from their industry/sector (I.e., as statistics, performance data etc).

- Established when to Measure KPI (I.e., it might be based on quarterly reporting or annual etc).

- Has developed a reporting format.

You can always leverage on reporting format others have already used and modify to fit your requirements (i.e., make it understandable for your leadership). **Why reinvent the wheel?**

Research and benchmarking against others who are on a similar journey will allow you to leverage on their lessons learned. **Why repeat mistakes?**

Indeed isolated KPI (i.e., ones that you have developed just for your Organisation) can and do help. However, only with a comparison with others and their performance can you enhance value and your motivation. **Success breeds competition.**

Let's expand our original table for Measurement Opportunities for Risk Management with potential Leading and Lagging indicators. This gives us a new table as below:

Measurement Opportunities for Risk Management with Leading and Lagging Indicators

Framework	Leading Indicator	Lagging Indicator
Policy	<ul><li>Development</li><li>Implementation</li><li>Effectiveness</li></ul>	<ul><li>Deviations</li></ul>
Attitude	<ul><li>Organisation's and individual manager's performance.</li></ul>	
Control	<ul><li>Developing details on nature and types of causes and consequences</li></ul>	<ul><li>The number of higher risks identified without management approval</li></ul>
HIRA	<ul><li>Effectiveness of risk treatment measures.</li><li>Critical equipment and procedures evaluated in a structured format utilising the risk assessment process</li><li>The number of operating procedures developed and documented, relative to the plan.</li></ul>	<ul><li>The number of risks assessments not conducted with personnel trained in techniques</li><li>The number of risk assessments, relative to the plan.</li></ul>
Actions Management	<ul><li>Progress in implementing risk</li></ul>	<ul><li>The number of outstanding risk</li></ul>

Framework	Leading Indicator	Lagging Indicator
	treatment by reviewing the Risk Register.	actions in Risk Registers
Performance Improvement	• Risk management performance against indicators	
Reviewing	• Continuous improvement in risk management	• Deviation from the Risk Management Plan • Number of accidents, incidents and near misses attributable to lack of or improper risk assessment

- Some of the measurements above could be just applied across many Elements (e.g., number of actions related to risk assessments).

- With measurement, there is potential to double, triple count etc.

- Measurement, Metrics and KPI provide a fertile ground for creativity, not only in selection but also in how they can be benchmarked and communicated within an Organisation.

We can conclude that:

- There is a reasonable argument in suggesting that some Metrics in the above table can be either Leading or Lagging.

- Metrics are prone to be subjective and similar

> to the "glass half empty or half full" analogy (e.g., metrics for attitude).
>
> - When we are looking at KPI of risk actions completed or not completed, my preference is for the latter. Focusing on completed actions is great, but I want to know about actions that are not completed since they make my Organisation vulnerable to risk exposure.

So, should you have Leading or Lagging KPI?

> - When selecting Metrics and differentiating for Leading and Lagging indicators, it's good practice to have a blend of Leading and Lagging indicators.
>
> - Being an iterative process, they can always be re-tuned or re-defined based upon experience and lessons learned.
>
> - **In my experience, I review every metric / KPI for sensitivity** I.e., a small negative increase in one indicator might outweigh the big positive increase in another.
>
> - The direction of travel and magnitude have to be taken into consideration when comparing Leading and Lagging KPI (from your Physics lessons, think of KPI as **Vectors - having direction as well as magnitude).**

Regardless of whichever measurement option is selected, the Organisation will have to set out bespoke Metrics, Leading and Lagging indicators that can be used for reviewing performance.

Leading and Lagging indicators work in harmony, supporting the Organisation in achieving goals and objectives.

KPI also play a vital role in communicating appropriate messages, both internally and externally. **So, handle with care!**

E5.6 How to Communicate KPI

There are a number of ways that risk management Leading and Lagging KPI can be communicated within an Organisation.

Performance indicators are discussed and reviewed at various levels within an Organisation. Reviews are regular standing items on the agenda for monthly or quarterly board meetings, operations meetings etc.

It's therefore important to get your message across effectively. We know that a visual representation of performance can be attention-grabbing and eye-catching.

I know that I am perhaps stating the obvious here, but when it comes to communicating KPI, the golden rule is to **keep it simple and consistent.**

Unfortunately, human nature being what it is, there is a tendency to focus more on negative aspects. Overcome this by placing emphasis on the positive results as well. It can't be all doom and gloom!

Your communication needs to accommodate negative and positive messages, without exaggerating and getting across key essential facts.

Remember, Measurement, Metrics and KPI provide a fertile ground for creativity not only in selection but also in how they can be benchmarked and communicated within an Organisation. **Leverage on this whenever possible**.

My own preference for effectively communicating KPI makes use of Heat Maps and Dashboards.

But what are Heat Maps and Dashboards?

Heat Map - What are they and how do I develop one?

A heat map is essentially a pictorial representation of values on a matrix, using colour.

You will recall that we are rather fortunate in having our colourful Risk Assessment Matrix based on traffic lights. We can very easily show the position of all the risks using this Risk Assessment Matrix.

 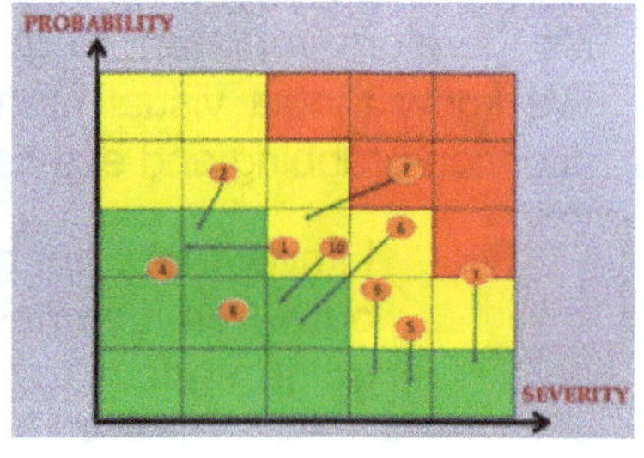

For example:
In the image adjacent, not only can we show where the risks are in relative terms but also the direction of travel over time. It's our **"Vector KPI"** approach.

Note that in this image…
- Probability = Likelihood
- Severity = Consequences

For your Heat Map, it's always a good idea to include a short narrative explaining specific features, with conclusions and recommendations. This minimises misinterpretation

Dashboards - What are they and how do I develop one?

Dashboards are very popular for communicating KPI, especially at executive board and leadership levels.

They are relatively easy to create plus equally quick in creating confusion with too many charts, numbers, bells and whistles.

Again, there are no specific rules regarding Dashboards.

A Dashboard essentially provides a specific focus on KPI taking into consideration your Leading and Lagging indicators.

Dashboards tend to be a "grid" type construct and can be anything from **2 x 2, 3 x 3, 4 x 4** etc.

The more grids, the greater the amount of data and the greater the potential for confusion.

For example:
In the image adjacent, we have a 2 x 2 Dashboard. We can even use our Heat Map as a Leading Indicator.

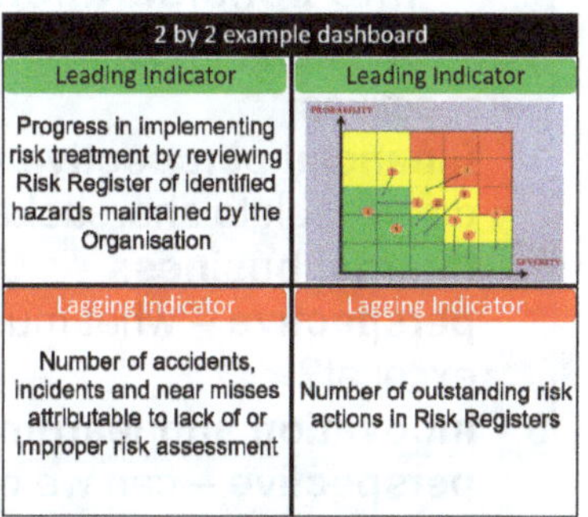

Other examples of Leading and Lagging indicators can be incorporated to fill the remaining panels, such as status on Risk Registers, KRI status, actions outstanding etc.

My suggestion is to start small (e.g., 2 x 2 matrix) and then expand as necessary. This will also allow others to catch up, understand and align with the overall Risk Management concepts.

Balanced Scorecards - What are they?

It would be unfair to not ***briefly*** mention Balance Scorecards (BSC). Created in 1992 by Robert Kaplan and David Norton, the BSC was initially aimed at helping public agencies better manage and measure performance.

More recently, BSC has been used for an integrated approach for performance measurement and management. It provides a measure of current performance and also the opportunity to "look forward", rather than backward (i.e., leading indicator as opposed to lagging indicator).

Some of the key attributes of BSC include:

Balance Scorecard attributes

What factors can they take into consideration?	How can they be used?
BSC can offer 4 important perspectives: 1. **Financial perspective** – how do we look to shareholders? 2. **Internal business perspective** – what must we excel at? 3. **Innovation and learning perspective** – can we continue to improve and create value? 4. **Customer perspective** – how do customers see us relative to time, quality, performance and service, and cost? By combining financial, internal process and innovation, Organisational learning and customer perspectives, the BSC help Organisational leaders better understand the interrelationships between the various facets.	BSC is most often used in three ways: • To bring an Organisation's strategy to life. • To communicate the strategy across the Organisation. • To track strategic performance.

What are their critical characteristics?	What's their capability?
The critical characteristics that define a BSC are: • Focus on the strategic agenda of the Organisation concerned. • The selection of a small number of data items to monitor. • A mix of financial and non-financial data items.`	With a Balanced Scorecard, you have the capability to: • Describe your strategy; and • Measure your strategy.

 You may recall we considered People as our impact category, especially as we are focusing on workplace and process hazards. But, it is also possible to cover impacts associated with other consequence categories such as financial, environment, stakeholders, public relations etc.

It's quite feasible that the above 4 BSC factors can also be incorporated into the Organisation's Risk Assessment Matrix and subsequently risk evaluation processes.

If you wish to scope out your Organisation's BSC, use the following as guidance:

- **Objectives**: Set high-level goals

- **Measures**: Define how to achieve the objective

- **Initiatives**: Are put in place to answer the question "what actions am I taking to accomplish the objective?

- **Actions**: Help that will allow you to complete your initiatives.

Addressing the above will give some assurance and confidence on whether BSC is a good method for communicating within your Organisation.

- If your Organisation already uses BSC and everyone is fairly familiar with what it means, then **adapt it for Risk Management and KPI communications**.
- Otherwise, start simple and then expand using Heat Maps and Dashboards.

- Avoid KPI overpowering and taking control of your Risk Management Framework.
- It can lead to "**paralysis by analysis**".

What should you monitor and what's the monitoring frequency?

E5.7 Monitoring and Monitoring Frequency

Risk never sleeps and risk management is "business as usual" on a continuous basis (I.e., there is no on/off switch).

Since monitoring plays an important and active supportive role, it stands to reason that monitoring is also a continuous activity.

Monitoring needs to be an integral part of your Risk Management Framework because it supports assurance via feedback. Hence, the Organisation must ensure that responsibilities for monitoring and review are clearly defined.

Knowing **what to monitor is relatively straight forward** since we have already established:

- What we are Measuring;

- Our Metrics; and

- Our Leading and Lagging KPI.

By monitoring and feeding results into the reporting and communication processes (I.e., Heat Map, Dashboard or Balanced Score Card), the Organisation can review the output at the appropriate management level, fine tune and provide support, if needed.

There are no hard and fast rules regarding frequency of monitoring and the Organisation might decide frequency based upon specific requirements.

<u>For example</u>:
The frequency of specific meetings can influence monitoring frequency
- The board meeting takes place quarterly and this could suggest monthly measurements.

- There might be regulatory requirements such as reporting of process risks due to legal obligations. In such cases, the frequency might be imposed by regulators.

On a cautionary note, achieving reporting should not be your baseline for setting monitoring frequency since monitoring is aimed at performance improvement.

<u>As a general rule of thumb</u>:
- Monitoring frequency can be split so as to allow periodic reviews and fine-tuning opportunities.

- The intention remains unaltered in that the purpose is to make sure the Risk Management Framework is effective in achieving and delivering the Organisation's objectives.

Organisations are and will always be in a state of flux. Monitoring KPI and frequency of monitoring will ensure that the Risk Management Framework is performing as intended.

4.8 ELEMENT 6: Reviewing

E6.1 Why Review?

Perhaps a nonsensical question, but **why carry out reviews?**

A review is defined as:

An activity undertaken to determine the suitability, adequacy and effectiveness of the subject matter to achieve established objectives.

Reviews can be carried out on the:

- Risk Management **Framework**;

- Risk Management **Policy** (functional aspects); and

- Risk Management **Plan** (arrangement aspects).

There are 2 distinct and separate types of reviews, namely:

1. **Formal Reviews** of the Risk Management Framework, Policy and Plan.

2. **Informal Reviews** of the framework, plan and results from monitoring (which is continuous by default).

Whilst the target audience might be different for the results from reviews, the intention of a review is to allow the Organisation to identify issues and implement improvement actions, if necessary.

Hence, reviews are unique and aimed at examining:

- The **performance** of the Risk Management Framework and how it compares to the established objectives; and

- The **effectiveness** of the Risk Management Framework in achieving the established objectives.

Poor quality reviews of performance and effectiveness will expose the Risk Management Framework to vulnerability and failure. This, in turn, will expose the Organisation to potential risks due to mismanagement.

Unfortunately, it is very easy to write an entire book on the subject of formal or informal reviews. In fact, many have been written.

In essence:

- Reviews provide feedback to the Organisation on the overall wellbeing of the Risk Management Framework.

- Review processes and mechanisms have to work functionally for the Organisation and meet set intentions (I.e., it's a part of the business mantra and not an add-on tick-box feature).

Organisations **must** establish clear guidelines, procedures, protocols, schedules and allocation of suitably qualified resources for conducting formal or informal reviews of their Risk Management Framework

It's also worth mentioning that there are several ISO Standards that offer guidance, protocols and requirements on review processes, especially **Audits**.

E6.2 Auditing the Risk Management Framework

Audits are **formal reviews** requiring a structured approach and methodology. They play a very important role as a review mechanism of the Risk Management Framework.

Audits are carried out using suitably qualified internal or external resources or they can even be conducted by regulators, as part of an Organisation's legal obligations and requirements. They are planned, use bespoke templates, procedures and defined protocols.

Audit results are reviewed at the highest level within the Organisation and can form part of the due-diligence or compliance process for assurance.

It is worth pointing out that formal reviews **are not just "audits"**. They can be a review conducted on a specific area or element, without following audit protocols e.g., an inspection.

Regardless of the type of Audit, careful planning and allocation of appropriately qualified resources are vitally important to ensure that the review quality is not compromised.

<u>Consider this example</u>:
If the Organisation has to meet a deadline for reporting and there is a delay, its' not uncommon to pick whoever is available for conducting the review. Although the intention was positive, the results can turn out to be quite negative. The entire review will be vulnerable to challenge and scrutiny.

Some of the key planning components for planning an Audit includes:

Planning an Audit

Before	During	After
• Setting the scope i.e. establishing the "ring-fence" on what is to be reviewed;	• Initial meeting - briefing individuals involved in the review process;	• Analysing information gathered from document reviews and interviews;
• Determining the method for gathering information (interview staff, make observations using a checklist, etc);	• Execution - Conducting the visit, utilising checklists and procedures, conducting interviews and probing for knowledge/ awareness of the Risk Management Framework;	• Preparing a report (draft) on what findings, including any improvement suggestions;
• Developing checklists and procedures for the review process to ensure that the process is rigorous;	• Verification - checking the existence of a policy, procedures etc., related to risk management;	• Providing a final report and feedback to Organisation; and
• Developing interview questions, as interviewing people play an important role during reviews; and	• Reviewing - registers, actions management	• Closeout final meeting with conclusions, recommendation s and what next.

Before	During	After
• Arranging dates, times and availability of appropriate people (I.e., who to visit, interview etc).	etc; • Validation - relative to performance improvement reports etc; and • Exit meeting - closeout meeting.	

CHAPTER 5: CLOSING THOUGHTS

It has been a **pleasure** and a **challenge** writing this book.

Pleasure in the sense that it made me dig deep into my experience and knowledge and share with you **only** what I consider to be essential in getting your Risk Management Framework established.

The **challenge** has been in deciding where to stop. It is so easy to venture deep into the risk management jungle and not "see the wood for the trees". **That is not "simplification"**.

You might already be on your risk management journey or you might be just starting? I do hope that the details, knowledge and experience shared via this book will aid and support you in that venture.

Before I sign off, I can only offer the following additional thoughts for your journey:

- ➤ **Communication** - it's important that risk management is not created and operated in an "ivory tower". Share throughout your Organisation in an inclusive way because that's the only way you will get engagement and also positive motivation.

- ➤ **Changes** - change is inevitable, especially in the world of workplace and process risks. Ensure that you have a robust, well-defined Management of Change process in place. Change management is "do or die" for any business.

- ➤ **Residual risk reviews** - periodically make sure risks are reviewed. I have mentioned this a number of times in the book because it's very easy to become complacent and forget what risks we are dealing with and where they are in relative terms to changes within the Organisation.

Thank you for sharing this part of the journey with me.

Good luck.

References

1. Copyright, Designs and Patents Act 1988:
    https://www.legislation.gov.uk/ukpga/1988/48/contents

2. Wikipedia: https://en.wikipedia.org/wiki/In_Salah

3. ISO Website: https://www.iso.org/iso-31000-risk-management.html

4. OECD: https://stats.oecd.org/glossary/detail.asp?ID=2360

5. EU recommendation 2003/36:
    http://ec.europa.eu/growth/smes/business-friendly-environment/sme-definition_en

6. The etymology of risk from Rolf Skjong
    [http://research.dnv.com/skj/Papers/etymology-of-risk.pdf]

Acronyms

Drowning in a sea of acronyms, abbreviations and jargon is not a good baseline for simplification.

Hence, I have kept my use of acronyms essential and limited to the following:

Acronym	Expanded
BSC	Balanced Score Cards
HAZID	**HAZ**ard **ID**entification
HIRA	Hazard Identification and Risk Assessment
HSE	Health, Safety and Environment
ISO	International Organisation for Standardisation
KPI	Key Performance Indicator
KRI	Key Risk Indicator
SMART	**S**pecific, **M**easurable, **A**chievable, **R**elevant and **T**imely
ToR	Terms of Reference

Glossary

Terminology	Definition
Consequences	Outcome of an event affecting objectives
Event	Occurrence or change of a particular set of circumstances.
Hazard	Source with a potential to cause injury and ill health.
Key Performance Indicator (KPI)	Measurable value showing how effectively an Organisation is achieving or progressing their defined objectives. KPIs are context-driven in that they can be driven by the Organisation's strategy and Risk Owners. Values can be compared against past performance data or benchmarked against other similar Organisations.
Key Risk Indicator (KRI)	An indicator that estimates the potential for some form of resource degradation using mathematical formulae or models.
Likelihood	Chance of something happening.
Measure	Is a fundamental, unit-specific term and tend to be number or value driven.
Metric	A more appropriate term for highly standardised measurements based on procedures, calculation methods and systems for generating a number. Metrics can be derived from one or more measures and tend to be goal or performance orientated.
Organisation	Person or group of people that has its own functions with responsibilities, authorities and relationships to achieve its objectives.
Process	Set of interrelated or interacting activities which transforms inputs and outputs.
Process Risk	Consequences (I.e., outcome) of an event (including changes in circumstances) and the associated chance of something happening

Terminology	Definition
	(I.e., likelihood or probability) associated with a set of interrelated or interacting activities which transforms inputs and outputs.
Residual Risk	Risk remaining after risk treatment (I.e., process to modify the risk).
Review	Activity undertaken to determine the suitability, adequacy and effectiveness of the subject matter to achieve established objectives.
Risk	Risk is a combination of the consequences (I.e., outcome) of an event (including changes in circumstances) and the associated chance of something happening (I.e., likelihood or probability)
Risk Analysis	Process to comprehend the nature of risk and to determine the level of risk.
Risk Appetite	Amount and type of risk that an Organisation is willing to pursue or retain.
Risk Assessment	Overall process of risk identification, risk analysis and risk evaluation.
Risk Attitude	Organisation's approach to assess and eventually pursue, retain, take or turn away from risk.
Risk Control	Measure (or process) that is modifying the risk.
Risk Criteria	Terms of reference against which the significance of a risk is evaluated.
Risk Evaluation	Process of comparing results of the risk analysis with Risk Criteria to determine whether the risk and/or its magnitude is acceptable or tolerable.
Risk Identification	Process of finding, recognising and describing risks.
Risk Level	Magnitude of risk or combination of risks, expressed in terms of the combination of consequences and their likelihood.
Risk Management	Coordinated activities to direct and control an Organisation with regard to risk.

Terminology	Definition
Risk Management Framework	Set of components that provide the foundations and Organisational arrangements for designing, implementing, monitoring, reviewing and continually improving risk management throughout the Organisation.
Risk Management Plan	Scheme within the risk management framework specifying the approach, the management components and resources to be applied to the management of risk.
Risk Management Policy	Statement of the overall intentions and direction of an Organisation related to risk management.
Risk Owner	Person or entity with the accountability and authority to manage a risk.
Risk Perception	Stake holder's view on a risk.
Risk Profile	Description of any set of risks
Risk Tolerance	An Organisation's or stockholder's readiness to bear the risk after risk treatment in order to achieve its objectives
Risk Treatment	Process to modify risk.
Risk Treatment Plan	Purpose is to document how the chosen treatment options will be implemented
Stakeholder	Person or Organisation that can affect, be affected by, or perceive themselves to be affected by a decision or activity.
Workplace	Place under the control of the Organisation where a person needs to be or to go for work purposes.
Workplace Risk	Consequences (I.e., outcome) of an event (including changes in circumstances) and the associated chance of something happening (I.e., likelihood or probability) in a place under the control of the organisation, where a person needs to be or to go for work purposes

About the Author

After graduating from the University of Bradford with a degree in Chemical Engineering, Sonni's working career began as a Process Engineer in Research and Development (R&D).

With a career spanning over 30 years, Sonni has held senior-level leadership roles in major multi-national Organisations. He has worked in excess of 40 countries and has a portfolio associated with Clients in the chemicals manufacturing, waste and energy management sector.

Sonni led the development, implementation and external ISO14001 certification of the first (Globally) Engineering, Procurement, Construction and Commissioning (EPCC) project for BP, valued in excess of $4Bn[2].

Sonni holds the following professional qualifications:

- **Fellowship**: Institution of Chemical Engineers (FIChemE)

- **Specialist Fellow**: International Institute of Risk and Safety Management (SFIIRSM)

- **Chartered Safety Practitioner**: Member of Institute of Occupational Safety and Health (CMIOSH).

- **Chartered Engineer**: Institution of Chemical Engineers (CEng).

- **Chartered Environmentalist**: Institution of Chemical Engineers (CEnv).

- **Certified Trainer**: Level 3 Award in Education and Training, AET.

You can find out more about Sonni's background on LinkedIn.

Index